D0966142

BEARER OF A MILLION DREAMS

BEARER OF A MILLION DREAMS

THE BIOGRAPHY OF THE

Statue of Liberty

Frank Spiering

Jameson Books

OTTOWA, ILLINOIS

Jameson Books are available at special discounts
for bulk purchases for sales promotions, premiums,
fund-raising, or educational use. Contact:

Jameson Books
722 Columbus Street
Ottawa, IL 61350

(815) 434-7905

Distributed by Kampmann and Company, New York City.

Printed in the United States of America

Designed by Irving Perkins

10   9   8   7   6   5   4   3   2   1

Contents

ACKNOWLEDGEMENTS

Many of us casually take for granted that the Statue of Liberty has always been there, serenely standing in the middle of New York harbor. We have learned to take much for granted, as we surrender ourselves to the stimulation of an era which urges us to refurbish, complicate and alter many aspects of our lives. It is not that we can no longer think for ourselves. It is that we are so inundated by the demands of materialism and peer pressure to achieve material prosperity that we are in pressing danger of losing that unique idealism which once made the United States of America the final hope of the world.

The word *liberty* or *liberté* is French in origin, deriving from the Latin, *libertat* or *libertas*. In Webster's Dictionary it is defined as the quality or state of being free, free from physical restraint, free from arbitrary or despotic control, the positive enjoyment of various social, political or economic rights and privileges, the power of choice.

The Statue of Liberty was not always there. There were surprising circumstances which brought it to this country. It grew out of seemingly chance meetings involving a number of brilliant people as well as certain events occurring at just the right moment. In fact, it almost did not happen at all.

Schoolchildren are taught that the Statue of Liberty was a gift from France. But they are seldom taught why the French gave us such a gift. They are not informed that a century ago there existed a few men and women with such passionate enthusiasm that they envisioned a monument that would last forever.

Within this book are the letters of Frederick Auguste Bartholdi, creator of the Statue, which he wrote from America, as well as letters from his wife, Jeanne-Emilie, and his mother, Charlotte, which have never before been published. I was permitted to reproduce them through the great kindness of Pierre Burger, conservateur de musée Bartholdi in Colmar, France.

No biography exists of the brilliant engineer, Gustave Eiffel. The details of his life and his work on the Statue of Liberty were recounted to me in Paris by his great granddaughter, Amelie Granet. Others in France who were extremely helpful were Michael Yvon, Jean Michel and Professor Gabriel Dupuy of the Ecole Nationale, Paris, Philippe Grand-jean, architect in charge of rebuilding the Statue of Liberty, Henry Loy-rette of the Musée D'Orsay, Françoise Reynaud, the Musée Carmavalet, Edmond Gerrer, Mayor of Colmar, Deputy Mayor Richard Riehm, Christian Kempf and Bertrand Lemoine.

In the United States I received valuable help from Herbert R. Hands of the American Society of Civil Engineers, Hughes de Kerret, cultural attaché, French Embassy, New York City, Priscilla Baker, United States Department of the Interior, Thierry Despont, Sherry Birk and Tony Wrenn of the American Institute of Architects, Lonnie Maguire, Carole L. Perrault, Architectural Conservateur, National Park Service, and Won H. Kim, Librarian for the American Museum of Immigration at the Statue of Liberty National Monument.

Little has been written about the life of the gifted poet Emma Lazarus and her romance with Washington Nathan. My research in this area was vastly assisted by Dr. Leonard Gold of the Jewish Division, New York Public Library, and Nathan M. Kaganoff, American Jewish Historical Society, Waltham, Massachusetts.

Adelaide Beaubier Webster, who translated from the French the hand-writing of the Bartholdis, was superlative in her efforts.

And finally my friend Freya Manston, who is a marvelous agent, in-spired me with her endless confidence and vision.

I dedicate to all of you this book, the realization of *my* dream.

Prologue

LIBERTÉ

"I knew a man once who after having visited countries where liberty and equality reigned, got it into his head to establish all that in his own country. Do you know what happened to him?" inquired Frederick the Great of Prussia. "No, sire," replied Lafayette. "He was hanged," Frederick said.

WHEN in October of 1782, the victorious Marquis de Lafayette returned to France from the thirteen colonies of America, he was greeted by a thunderous uproar. Thousands of his fellow countrymen stood in the streets and along the boulevards of Paris tearfully and joyously acclaiming him "the hero of two worlds." Fishwives presented the dashing twenty-eight-year-old marquis with laurel wreaths, and the most beautiful woman in Paris, Mme. de Simiane, publicly offered to make love to him. At the opera they sang about him, a dinner was given for him by the marshals of France, and on that same evening, at a ball in his honor at the Palais Royal, he danced the quadrille with Queen Marie-Antoinette.

For five years Lafayette had helped the Americans fight for and win their independence. In the words of Diderot, "The principles of liberty and independence formerly hidden in the heart of a few thinkers had now become established and were openly rec-

ix

ognized." America had freed itself from the whims of tyrants, embracing in its Declaration of Independence that most precious apothegm—"life, liberty and the pursuit of happiness. . . ."

Lafayette wanted the same for France.

The spirit of revolution had been kindled in France, but the Bastille, the ancient symbol of royal suppression, still stood in the center of Paris at the mouth of the Boulevard St. Martin. Here opponents of the king could be imprisoned by *lettres de cachet* for years at a time, without benefit of formal charges or a trial.

Finally, on July 14, 1789, the Bastille was razed by revolutionary forces. Lafayette gave the key to the Bastille to George Washington, and Washington kept it at his home in Mount Vernon.

France was suddenly aflame with idealism. Lafayette was held in such esteem that the National Assembly appointed him commander-in-chief of the French armies. At the same time he gave France a new flag: the blue, white, and red tricolor.

But Lafayette was to be haunted by the words of a Boston clergyman. As the French troops were leaving America at the end of the Revolutionary War in 1782, the Reverend Samuel Cooper had bid them adieu with a chilling prophecy: "You will carry our sentiments with you, but if you try to plant them in a country that has been corrupt for centuries, you will encounter obstacles more formidable than ours. Our liberty has been won by blood. You will have to shed it in torrents."

Two weeks after the fall of the Bastille a certain old man, Foullon, was dragged from his home by a crowd of revolutionaries for supposedly cornering the wheat market. He had apparently remarked, "The people ought to be happy enough to be given straw to eat."

A frenzied mob brought the wretched old man to the Hotel de Ville where Lafayette attempted to reason with them. There was a sudden hush as the young marquis spoke. "I am known to you all—you have made me your commander . . . I must speak to you with all the liberty and frankness for which I am known . . . I insist that the law be respected, that law without which there can be no liberty, without which I could not have shared in the revolution of the new world, without which I cannot share in this revolution. I command that this man be taken to the prison of St. Germain for trial."

For minutes Lafayette struggled with the mob for the life of the old man.

At last many began to applaud Lafayette's words.

Suddenly someone saw the idiotic Foullon join in the clapping and shouted: "Look! The two have an understanding!"

The old man was seized, dragged out, and butchered.

To make matters worse, Bertier, Foullon's son-in-law, was fetched and hacked to death by a hundred blows.

In the evening the drunken throngs crowded around the pikes upon which were impaled the heads of Foullon and his son-in-law, and as the bleeding remains knocked together, they shouted coarsely: "Kiss papa! Kiss papa!" Gouverneur Morris, one of the signers of the United States Constitution, who was watching from afar, commented, "Gracious God! What a people!"

On the morning of October 5, 1789, three months after the fall of the Bastille, the dregs of Paris gathered outside the Hotel de Ville. "To Versailles!" they began to shout.

By evening, a crowd of women had descended upon the palace of Versailles like a swarm of insects screaming in fury at the queen. "I'll have her thighs!" shouted one. "I'll have her insides!" shrieked another.

At 10:00 P.M. Lafayette and his guard arrived.

The vigil of the mob in front of the palace continued throughout the night. At 5:00 A.M. a gate into the palace was mysteriously unlocked. Into it poured a horde of the most bloodthirsty members of the crowd. The queen's guard fired as the mob attacked, killing half a dozen and wounding twenty others.

The assassins were unstoppable. They raced up the palace stairs.

Darting from her bedchamber, the queen attempted to flee as the intruders shouted that they had come to cut out her liver.

In terror, Marie-Antoinette dashed through the antechamber and managed to escape from her petits appartements into the two hundred and thirty-five-foot long Gallerie des Glaces, where she was joined by her husband, Louis XVI.

Lafayette rushed into the Gallerie, just in time to save the royal family. But the real danger was only beginning. The mob outside the palace began to howl. There was no guarantee that the palace guards would try to resist them.

Lafayette made a desperate choice. "Come with me and show

yourself to the people." He beckoned to the queen.

Marie-Antoinette shuddered at the specter of those ghastly, hating faces. "Go to the balcony alone? Did you see what signs they were making?"

"Come." Gently Lafayette led her through Louis XIV's bed-chamber, out onto the balcony overlooking the Cour de Marbre. They were greeted with a roar. The crowd looking up were struck with awe to see their beautiful, pale, half-dressed queen. Lafayette took her hand, which trembled with cold and fear, and with a low bow, kissed it.

"Vive le general! Vive la reine!" the crowd suddenly began to shout.

Lafayette's gesture had succeeded. The crowd's anger suddenly turned to cheers.

On July 14, 1790, the first anniversary of the fall of the Bastille, a Festival of Federation was held in the center of Paris. Standing at a national altar constructed in the field of the Champ-de-Mars, Lafayette swore an oath of loyalty to the law and the nation.

An enormous crowd of three hundred thousand solemnly re-peated the oath with him.

Louis XVI, watching from a nearby window, was so caught up in the general excitement that he suddenly joined in.

From England, Horace Walpole wrote: "M. de Lafayette gov-erns France instead of their King."

With the help of his friend, Thomas Jefferson, who had been appointed American minister to France, Lafayette drafted a Eu-ropean declaration of rights, based upon the principles of liberty. Its precepts echoed those that Jefferson had devised for the thir-teen colonies of America: "Every man is born with inalienable and imprescriptive rights, such as the right to the liberty of his opin-ions, the care of his honor and his life, the right to property . . ."

Unanimously it was adopted by the French Assembly.

A day later the work of Lafayette and Jefferson was circulated all over Paris.

In the months that followed, instead of the establishment of a constitutional government based on liberty, one form of oppres-sion was ruthlessly replaced by another. Under Robespierre, the commissioner of public safety, the mob became the government.

Sunday, January 21, 1793, was the day of the first execution. The guillotine was erected near the black grille gate leading to the Tuileries Gardens. At noon, Louis XVI, brought from the Rue Royale, climbed the steps of the scaffold. Above the roll of the drums, he attempted to make his last words heard by the populace waiting below.

> My people, I die innocent of the serious crimes of which I am accused . . . may my blood consolidate the happiness of France.

The king was strapped to a perpendicular oak plank. The plank was then lowered until it was horizontal and was run along grooves into position under the knife.

The drums stopped.

With the fall of the "nation's razor," the Reign of Terror had begun.

Marie-Antoinette was tried. The prosecutor Hebert charged that she had committed improper acts with her eight-year-old son. Although Robespierre cursed him angrily, Hebert pressed the improbable charge.

The queen replied, "I appeal to the hearts of all mothers present."

Marie-Antoinette's two children were dragged from her arms and she was never allowed to see them again. No longer resembling the beautiful young woman whose hand Lafayette had kissed on the balcony at Versailles, by the time she was taken to the area near the black grille gate leading to the Tuileries Gardens, she was so frail she could hardly walk.

The blade thundered across her neck.

As Sanson, the executioner, held up her bloody head, whose eyelids still quivered convulsively, the immense crowd cried, "Vive la République!"

In August 1793 Lafayette himself was imprisoned, where he remained until he was released by Napoleon I five years later.

Even though the events in this book begin eighty years after his imprisonment, the spirit of Lafayette moves through them, his courageous presence guiding those who came after. Lafayette knew that France's solution was not the overturning of the government and the murder of its king and queen. He envisioned a dedication to the spirit of Liberty such as Europe had never known—

The only non-American whose portrait hangs in the halls of the United States Congress is Lafayette. There is also a lifelike statue of Lafayette standing in Manhattan's Union Square, overlooked by the crowds hurrying by. The young marquis is seen as a tall, handsome, heroic figure. His face and eyes still glow with idealistic dreams of Liberty. His right hand presses his sword to his chest, as if making a passionate vow. Beneath his feet are engraved the words:

As soon as I heard of American Independence
My heart was enlisted

On the opposite side of the pedestal is the inscription:

To the City of New York
France
In Remembrance of Sympathy in Time of Trial
1870 - 1871

Most people who pass are unaware that the creator of the Lafayette statue is Auguste Bartholdi, the same sculptor who is represented by yet another statue, famous throughout the world, which stands a few miles to the west—the magnificent, mighty figure of a lady.

PART
I

The Artist

Auguste Bartholdi

THE FIVE-MILE route down Fifth Avenue to Broadway was a vast sea of soggy bunting and French tricolors. It was Thursday, October 28, 1886, the day that the Statue of Liberty was to be unveiled in New York harbor.

American stars and stripes hung from doorways and rooftops as over a million people elbowed against each other to watch the biggest parade in New York City's history. The marchers set off at 9:00 A.M. at Fifth Avenue and Fifty-seventh Street, strode down Fifth Avenue to Washington Square to Broadway, and then on down Broadway to the Battery.

World leaders vied with one another for seats of prominence in the Madison Square reviewing stand at Twenty-third Street and Fifth Avenue. Twenty thousand individual units passed by the reviewing stand, including members of the armed forces, volunteer fire department, police force, fraternal organizations, the Grand Army of the Republic, the Grenadiers Rochambeau, the Société Israelite, and the Garde Lafayette. Bands of every description, school groups, patriotic societies, nearly every resident of the city who was not watching the parade was marching through the rain.

At 1:00 P.M. on the Hudson River there was a naval procession of the Atlantic Squadron. Through it all, the French sculptor Auguste Bartholdi waited inside the brown, copper-plated head of the Statue of Liberty. The island below him had filled with the richest, most famous men in America.

Bartholdi's brown eyes were intense, his face was lined with exhaustion and excitement. His wiry body leaned against an interior section of the monument's mighty crown as he anxiously looked down through the ten-foot diadem windows at New York harbor. The waters churned with tiny boats, little sail craft, superb private yachts, huge-tonnaged merchant steamers, and thundering ironclads, lying side by side with pleasure craft and little screaming tugs sending forth their shrill signals. The vision he had lived with since he was a young man was about to come true. It had cost him a fortune. It had taken fifteen years of his life.

But Bartholdi's passion for his dream had forced him onward, never allowing him to forget the summer morning, years before, when he first entered that same harbor. What appeared before him then was a vision of a statue that would stand forever.

Just as all the avenues of Paris led to the gleaming Arc de Triomphe, built before he was born, so all the people he had met—Edouard de Laboulaye, Gustave Eiffel, John La Farge, Joseph Pulitzer—had led him to this moment.

The Statue of Liberty would make the name *Auguste Bartholdi* world famous. He was only seconds away from its unveiling.

There was a sudden ear-shattering, twenty-one-gun salute. The president of the United States had stepped onto the shore of the island. The smoke from the guns rose, mingling with the rain and thick fog, so that Auguste could no longer make out what was happening.

He was to pull the cord releasing the French flag at a signal from a boy on the ground three hundred feet below.

But he could no longer see the boy.

There was cannon fire. Auguste tugged the unveiling cord. The huge tricolor fell aside. The ships around the island began to blast whistles. Guns roared in salute. Bands began to play. The people below cheered.

The Statue's face bore the likeness of the face of his mother, Charlotte. She had seldom left the town of Colmar, in the province of Alsace, where he had been born and raised, yet she had guided his life.

His mother had always been there, even on that night fifteen years before . . . at the beginning . . .

1

Charlotte Bartholdi

I am looking at the stars . . . then my mind wanders, and I think that I see you far away beyond the horison.
>   —AUGUSTE BARTHOLDI, in a let-
>   ter to his mother from Egypt,
>   1869

FOR WEEKS Bismarck's Prussian armies had been preparing to invade Alsace, on the eastern border of France. The time had finally come. It was October 1, 1870.

That evening Charlotte Bartholdi climbed the winding stairs of her four-story house on rue des Marchands in Colmar. From the top floor she would be able to watch her son Auguste leading a column of French soldiers through the town. There had been no doubt in her mind that Auguste would become one of France's greatest sculptors. But now, suddenly, at the height of his artistic powers, he had enlisted as a major in the French army.

Charlotte was a large woman, sixty-nine years of age, yet her face bore few wrinkles. She had a long, delicate neck, a firm jaw, and penetrating grey eyes. Her dark brown hair was combed into soft curls partially hidden beneath a black lace veil.

Her large house, built of white stone, was located in the center of town. It was cared for by Charlotte's two servants, a maid and a handyman.

Charlotte had lived in Colmar since her marriage to Jean-Charles Bartholdi when she was twenty-eight. Her husband had been a prosperous landowner and a member of the city council. The Bartholdis had come from Frankfurt, where the family name had originally been Barthold. In 1712, Charlotte's husband's great-grandmother, Marie Dorothee Barthold, had latinized it, changing the name to Bartholdi to make it sound more romantic and fashionable.

In 1836, eight years after their marriage, Charlotte's husband died, leaving her to raise their two sons, Charles and Auguste. One son was to become a constant source of pain and regret, the other her joy.

The older, Charles Bartholdi, appeared to have a splendid future as a painter. He was a handsome young man, a dandy of the town, who had studied in Paris in the studio of the famous landscape artist Ary Scheffer. And then, in his early thirties, a scandal surfaced that nearly cost Charlotte Bartholdi everything she possessed.

Charles had secretly fallen in love with a young woman named Fanny Dreyfus.

There were two obstacles to the love affair: Fanny was married and she was Jewish. Although Charlotte was unaware of her son's love affair, she had observed his agitation, and when his actions became erratic she had his brother Auguste take him to see a doctor in Basel. On the way, Charles began to sob. When Auguste tried to comfort him, Charles became murderous. Grabbing Auguste by the throat, he attempted to throw him off the train. Within days, Charlotte was presented with three promissory notes which Charles had signed. The total value of the notes, held by Fanny's brother, Mark Dreyfus, was a small fortune.

Charlotte called a tribunal and asked to be appointed her son's guardian, thus allowing her to claim that the promissory notes were void, that his signature had been obtained by trickery as he was mentally unbalanced. She demanded that Charles be certified legally insane and deprived of his civil rights. During the proceedings, it was revealed that Fanny Dreyfus had had adulterous relations with him for a period of twelve years.

Charles was committed to a rest home near Paris. In the years that followed, Charlotte, filled with remorse, attempted to keep in touch with her older son, writing him constantly, begging him to write.

Charles never responded.

The focus of her love and attention in the last years of her life became her youngest son, Auguste. Frederic Auguste was his formal name, but the Frederic was never used, just as her husband, Jean-Charles, had been known simply as Charles.

In Paris, Auguste had studied to become a sculptor. With enormous energy and enthusiasm, he set ambitious goals for himself. Eagerly he pursued the city's artistic life, making influential friends who admired his talent and helped him. By the time he was in his early twenties, Auguste's work was known all over France. He was commissioned to create monuments picturing some of the country's most prominent men—G.B. Lorentz, founder of the Academy of Forestry, Arrighi, the celebrated Corsican general, Martin Schongauer, the painter, and Marshal Georges Vauban. But it was on a three-month trip to Egypt in 1856, when he was twenty-two, that his romantic sensibility was overcome by dreams of glory.

As he wandered amidst the massive stone monuments of Thebes and Abu Simbel, he wrote to his mother that he was "filled with profound emotion in the presence of these colossal witnesses, centuries old . . . these granite beings, in their imperturbable majesty seem to be still listening to the most remote antiquity. Their kindly and impassible glance seems to ignore the present and be fixed upon an unlimited future . . . the design itself expresses infinity."

The images of those great faceless statues would never leave him. He vowed in his diary that one day he would create a monument that would be as striking and unforgettable, in which "the design itself" would express "infinity."

But within another decade France had changed. There were no commissions for great public monuments. Under Napoleon III, France had become a police state.

On the evening of October 1, 1870, when she reached the top floor of her house, Charlotte Bartholdi paused beside the hand-operated dumbwaiter, which had been constructed to lower food to the first-floor dining room. Through the windows she could see down to the winding streets below. A chill, blustering wind pressed hard against the stark, flat yellow fields surrounding the defenseless town of Colmar. Everywhere was the silent tenseness of dread, of waiting.

It was dusk. The darkening sun floated above the murky, distant hills dotted with thin criss-crossing furrows and black boughs laden with sour green grapes soon to ripen and fill mammoth oaken vats with dry Alsatian Riesling. The market place surrounding the ancient church of St. Martin was already deserted, yet the empty wooden stalls retained the rich smells of sausage casings stuffed with veal and steaming pork, tureens of goose liver and duck, enormous wheels of gruyere cheese, wooden barrels of sauerkraut, and fermenting brown beer.

By 7:00 A.M., the dark sun would be gone. A full moon would match the pale coolness of the autumn fields. Colmar would become quiet, beautifully still, not like a place where wars begin.

Yet, from the east the Prussian hordes of Bismarck were advancing. From the west the armies of Napoleon III swarmed to meet them. Within hours, scores of Krupp cannons would roar from the Haut-Rhin across the borders of Alsace, and the town of Colmar with its 26,000 inhabitants would shudder through the dark night.

Below her, the pottery and leather shops and the fine, old shuttered residences with their long, dark windows lined the narrow streets. From her fourth-story window, Charlotte watched her son Auguste lead the blue column of French soldiers from the old section of town, down the Street of Skulls, toward the square in which the statue of General Jean Rapp stood. It was her son, Frederic Auguste Bartholdi, who had created this monument to one of Napoleon I's most valiant generals. Rapp had distinguished himself at the Battle of Austerlitz, in which Napoleon defeated the combined armies of Austria and Russia. The statue was a lifelike representation—Rapp stood, legs and shoulders pitched forward with heroic determination, dressed in high boots and military jacket, with sword raised, about to rush into battle.

When Auguste built the statue, its height of more than twenty-five feet, with pedestal, was much too large to be exhibited in the Salon at Paris, so at first it had been placed in front of a building on the Avenue des Champs Elysées.

The Parisian press constantly wrote about it, referring to what they called its "colossal" proportions. Because General Rapp was a son of Colmar, as was the statue's creator Auguste Bartholdi, the people of Colmar finally claimed the statue for themselves.

When the bronze figure was unveiled in Colmar in 1856, it was the proudest day of Charlotte Bartholdi's life. She watched as Auguste, at the age of twenty-two, was presented the ribbon of knight in the Legion of Honor. There had been no doubt in her mind that he was destined to become one of France's greatest sculptors, that he would wipe away the disappointment of his elder brother, Charles. But now, suddenly, at the height of his artistic powers, he had enlisted as a major in the French army.

The huge bells in the steeple of St. Martin's had begun to toll. Terror filled Charlotte Bartholdi's heart as she watched the distant, uniformed figure of her son marching before the famous bronze statue he had created. Other bells joined in—from the Church of the Dominicans, the old Franciscan Church, the Church of St. Peter and Paul, of St. Leger, the ancient Benedictine church of Sainte-Foy—a thunder of bells . . . the final hope of her life, Auguste, was on his way to join the Italian patriot Garibaldi at Autun. He had been ordered by the government of Napolean III to fight a battle from which he might never return.

2

Napoleon III

PERSONALLY, PRUSSIAN Chancellor Otto von Bismarck felt no animosity toward France's ruler, Napoleon III. He admitted that he felt sorry for him because he was so foolish.

Dressed constantly in his white uniform, Bismarck was smoothly masterminding Germany's attempts to dominate Europe. In his memoirs he attempted to justify his invasion of France: "The moment had arrived when France sought a quarrel against us and was ready to seize any pretext that seemed available . . . France intended to threaten us with war."

Bismarck's rationalization was a lie, the French had no such intention. The sole cause of the Franco-Prussian war was Bismarck's own desire to extend Germany's borders.

The architect of the war was Prussian Chief of Staff Carl Bernhard von Moltke. After being humiliated in their war with Austria in 1866, the Prussians badly needed a military victory. To make the prospect of war more appealing, Moltke had suggested in a letter to Bismarck that once France was defeated and a peace treaty executed, "If the provinces of Alsace and Lorraine were conquered it is conceivable that we might keep them."

Seizing Alsace-Lorraine became Bismarck's prime goal and he conjured up an intricate scheme to bring it about. Aware that France and Spain were linked politically as well as geographically, he inveigled the Spaniards to invite a member of the German royalty, Prince Leopold, to be their king. Not only did the French regard this as Prussian interference in the sphere of interest, but, as it would result in their being bordered on two sides by the German monarchy, they immediately proclaimed it a threat to their security.

Napolean III ordered King William I of Prussia to withdraw his brother, Leopold, as a candidate for Spain's monarchy. William I refused. In fury, Napoleon III declared war on Prussia.

All along, Bismarck had skillfully anticipated how Napoleon III would react; he knew the French ruler's history.

Since his childhood, exiled in Switzerland, as a result of the fall of Napoleon I in 1815, Charles-Louis Napoleon Bonaparte had lived under the spell of his famous uncle. His contemporaries recalled that as a young man he had blond hair, blue eyes and the Bonaparte short legs; in addition, he had the misfortune to speak French with a German accent. He was extremely intelligent but seldom frank, and a highly manipulative opportunist. As an associate observed, "He was as great as a man can be without virtue."

When he was twenty-four he wrote a pamphlet, "Rêveries po-litiques," in which he asserted that only an emperor could give France both glory and power. Although he longed to follow in his uncle's footsteps and become that emperor, he possessed none of his uncle's abilities as a commander or statesman.

Backed by his family's political allies, he tried several times to take over the French government. Finally, in 1848 when he ran for president of France, his arrest was ordered by members of the National Assembly but the order was annulled by Conservatives who chose him as their candidate. Using the power of his name, he attempted to captivate French voters.

Evoking the Napoleonic legend with its memories of national glory, he promised to bring back those days in time of peace. Touring the provinces he was met with cries of "Vive l'Empereur." He found the greeting intoxicating. He appealed to every class of people, promising "protection" to the rich, "prosperity" to the middle class and "assistance" to the poor. He won by a substantial margin, being the only candidate to obtain votes from all of the nation's classes.

On December 19, 1848, when "Citizen Louis Bonaparte" was formally announced as president, he swore "to remain faithful to the democratic Republic and to defend the Constitution." He then moved into the Elysee Palace, where his uncle had lived, and began to plot how he, too, would become emperor.

In 1852, when he wished to run again, he was blocked by the Constitution which forbade the re-election of a president. Although Louis-Napoleon was a timid man who shrank from bloodshed, he organized a coup d'état. Fifty police patrols swept through the city arresting leaders of the National Assembly. When the Republicans resisted, there was bloody street fighting. Two hundred Republicans were arrested and sent to Devil's Island. Deportations numbered in the thousands.

Ruthlessly, Louis-Napoleon dissolved the National Assembly and decreed a new constitution. On December 2, 1852, before the altar of St. Cloud where Napoleon I had been crowned, he was proclaimed Napoleon III, emperor of the French.

During his ensuing eighteen-year reign, France was reduced to a second-rate power. The emperor was a political opportunist who maintained an authoritarian regime with a one-party government. After seizing power, he established a police state—any opposition was considered disloyal and potentially insurrectionary. He controlled the parliament and censored the press.

Twelve special commissaires were stationed in Paris and in other large cities to survey printing, including the book trade, and the selling of brochures and almanacs. Further, under the guise of protecting the state from subversion, another commission was positioned at the frontier points to examine and confiscate all imported printed material that might undermine civil order. When Abraham Lincoln was assassinated, there was such grief in France that a public subscription was immediately begun for a gold medal to be presented to Lincoln's widow. Napoleon III, fearing that such a gesture would appear supportive of democratic government, had his commissaires destroy the list of subscribers and seize the money.

What the emperor did encourage was the vulgarization of

French civilization. It was an age of conformity, close-mindedness, and superficial moral values.

Writers and painters were the greatest threat—they stirred up ideas. Both Flaubert *(Madame Bovary)* and Baudelaire *(Les Fleurs de Mal)* were arrested when their books were published. Ernest Pinard, the public prosecutor who conducted the case for the king, charged that *Madame Bovary* was a work of realism and therefore obscene. Going on to attack Baudelaire, Pinard's words became an indictment of every serious artist who ever lived: "He delves into the innermost recesses of human nature; he uses, to render it, strong and striking tones; he particularly exaggerates the hideous aspects; he magnifies inordinately so as to create the impression, the sensation."

The realist paintings of Gustave Courbet were criticized as ugly, their ideas dangerous. But the most scathing assault was reserved for the paintings of Edouard Manet. Not only were they condemned by the royalist press, but the jury of the Paris Exhibition of 1868 would not allow them even to be shown. Emile Zola commented that Manet had been treated like "a pariah, an unpopular and grotesque painter . . . an artist whom people pretend not to understand and who is banished from the little world of painters like a leper." Zola added, "If I had the cash I would buy every canvas Manet would sell me . . . in ten years time they will fetch fifteen or twenty times the price."

Napoleon III was powerless to silence one voice. From England, the self-exiled Victor Hugo unleashed a stream of denunciation. In *Les Chatiments,* Hugo compared Napoleon III to a thief and a highwayman, and in a pastiche of a La Fontaine fable, the emperor was presented as an obnoxious chimpanzee, dressed up in the moth-eaten costume of a tiger. As all of Europe joined with Hugo in jeering at the French emperor, the size of Hugo's popularity in France so increased that he was able to ask his publisher, Lacroix, for the record sum of three hundred thousand francs for the rights to his long-awaited novel, *Les Misérables.* Upon publication, the emperor could not stop the book's distribution. Immediately, it sold more than a half a million copies. The critic Sainte-Beuve remarked that Hugo "had won the greatest success of the age, stolen from under the nose of an extremely powerful government."

Hugo became the conscience of France. For twenty years he was to live as an exile in England as he attempted to awaken his countrymen. Surrounded by other exiles, such as Edmund and Jules de Goncourt, Hugo swore never to set foot again on his native land until the Empire had fallen and the Republic had been reestablished. Even if all his fellow refugees allowed themselves to be tempted by offers of amnesty, he vowed, "If there remain but ten, I shall be one of ten. If only one be left, that one will be myself."

Hugo prophesied a day of reckoning. He insisted that France's greatest threat was the emperor himself.

Napoleon III's earliest ambition had been to be a soldier like his famous uncle—an ambition that had only grown as he watched his nation deteriorate. Because of vanity and a self-centered thirst for glory, he finally blundered into war—with the greatest military power Europe had ever seen.

Bismarck had suffered severe losses in the war with the Austrians in 1866. He had subsequently honed and conditioned his troops, arming them with the most modern weapons—breach-loading cannons and the newly invented Mauser rifles.

Napoleon III was sixty-three years of age. On the morning he marched from Versailles to take command of the French armies gathered in Alsace-Lorraine, he was so ill with kidney stones that it took three strong men to lift his decadent, fat body onto a horse. Even though he confessed that he was unable to read a military map to assess the positions of his troops, his advisors had flattered him into believing that he was a military genius.

The emperor had equally deluded himself into believing that he had a standing force of eight hundred thousand, when, in reality, the French had a mere sixty thousand trained reservists. Among them was a thirty-six-year-old sculptor from Colmar, Auguste Bartholdi.

3

Bartholdi at War

MAJOR AUGUSTE BARTHOLDI stared across the Arroux River at the grey limestone tower, the ancient temple of Janus, the two-faced god of all beginnings. From this vantage point at the top of a hill in eastern France, he could study the troop fortifications below. His full black hair, parted neatly on the left, cleft chin, and thin, well-trimmed mustache made him appear handsome and aloof. His slim body was attired in the long blue uniform coat of the French National Guard, with gold epaulets and an officer's sword.

A year ago, in the spring of 1869, he had been in Egypt with Ferdinand de Lesseps, the great engineer who had constructed the Suez Canal. He had been there to design a lighthouse which would stand at the entrance to the newly completed waterway. It had been his second trip to Egypt. His first, in 1856, when he was twenty-two, had filled him with such visions of gigantic monuments and colossal figures that his artistic vision forevermore would focus upon what he called "the grand manner . . . The subject shall be grand, as are battles, heroic actions and divine things . . . "

Filled with ambition, Bartholdi had designed a lighthouse for the entrance to the Suez Canal in the form of a woman holding a torch, the theme being "Egypt carrying the light to Asia."

When de Lesseps saw Auguste's sketch for the lighthouse, he encouraged him. But Auguste's pursuit of greatness was frustrated by the khedive of Egypt, Ismail Pasha, who vetoed the project. Dejected, Auguste returned to his home in Colmar.

Auguste was thirty-five. His life as an artist had begun happily, as a nineteen-year-old student in Paris. There he met his lifelong friend, the American painter John la Farge. La Farge returned to New York, while Auguste stayed in France to create statues commemorating several of France's greatest men, for which, at twenty-two, he was commended by the Legion of Honor.

Even though he was a determined man, his potential, which seemed so promising at twenty-two, had not been fully realized. At this moment in his life, following his return from Suez, France declared war on Germany.

Auguste had been assigned quartermaster to a force of five thousand men stationed fifty miles southwest of Dijon, at Autun, the old Duchy of Burgundy. It was a small, ornate city, which stood on a hill enclosed by a Roman fortress.

Once, Autun had been an important Roman outpost. In the

third century, it was famous for its school of rhetoric. What remained were its Roman walls; the town had shrunk, receding behind them, until it harbored only the ancient medieval cathedral of St. Lazare.

Commanding the small army was the famed master of guerrilla warfare, Giuseppe Garibaldi. Now a white-haired old man, scarred by bullet wounds and so infirm with gout that he was hardly able to walk, Garibaldi had offered his services to rescue France from destruction.

All his life Garibaldi had been a man of war, fighting the most bloody kind of war, thrusting soldiers into battle against overwhelming, murderous odds. Unable to bear seeing a person or an animal in pain, he fervently opposed capital punishment. Yet, as one of his soldiers observed, he was capable of ordering them to be shot without putting down his cigar.

Only ten years before, his conquest of Sicily and Naples seemed the achievement of a demi-god. Afterward, his name was on everyone's lips. Throughout Europe young women dressed themselves in red blouses—the Garibaldian uniform. Plaster likenesses of him were sold by the thousands in Rome, Paris, London, Scandinavia. Men and women rejoiced in his stirring vision—freedom of thought, of civilization, the brotherhood of nations. . . .

Napoleon III had been stunned when Garibaldi offered him his services. Although Garibaldi hated the policies of the emperor, he was convinced that the French people had to be saved.

Garibaldi had described the war as a struggle of democracy against the forces of a reactionary monarchy—which would end in the liberation of mankind from the chains of feudalism. From Scotland his friend and great admirer John McAdam had urged him not to go to France, a country which had never come to the aid of Italy except to serve its own purposes. Garibaldi had replied: "I think that the democracies of all the nations must help the French Republic." He envisioned that one day France would overthrow its emperor and become a Republic.

Garibaldi's forces were volunteers, Italian, Polish, Hungarian revolutionaries, as well as members of the French National Guard and radicals who had once been political prisoners. Who else might believe as he did, that France must be saved not only from the Prussians but from the corruption of its own imperial regime?

It was a strange role for Garibaldi to play. It was almost as if he were leading an army of the future, disconnected with the policies of an existing government. It was only because Napoleon III became so desperate that he had reluctantly allowed him to fight for France.

Initially the great master of guerrilla warfare was to join the emperor's army at Dijon, but he refused to go—not until his volunteers were treated with the respect accorded to regular soldiers. He demanded that they be transported there by train.

Napoleon III rebuked him furiously, but at last agreed to supply him with a train.

When Garibaldi arrived at Dijon he ordered his men to use bayonets. By evening both sides had suffered enormous casualties but they stopped the Prussian advance. Garibaldi returned to Autun, undefeated, grimly awaiting the next confrontation that he knew was coming.

The unyielding, mythic figure of Garibaldi was someone Bartholdi would never forget. That they had been positioned to face the overwhelming superiority of Bismarck's armies was never mentioned by Auguste in his letters to his mother. "I am helping when I can those who are suffering. I am providing for the needs of poor soldiers. The day before yesterday I was able to obtain mercy for an Italian that they were going to execute by shooting." Not wishing to worry Charlotte Bartholdi, Auguste pretended that he was stationed behind the lines, employed as a clerk:

> If I do not carry a gun and I am not a warrior, at least I am useful . . . I have my small mission, which is not yet finished . . . If I were not separated from you, everything would be perfect.

By June 5, 1871, most of the French army had collapsed—Alsace-Lorraine was overrun by Prussian troops—but Garibaldi's small force held its position at Autun. Auguste knew that within hours the final assault of shellfire would begin.

In Paris, a desperate struggle was raging for control of the French government. Spearheaded by the courageous Republican Senator Edouard de Laboulaye, it would soon involve Auguste, not as a soldier, but as an artist executing his most famous commission.

4

The Plan for Liberty

SENATOR EDOUARD de Laboulaye was fifty-nine years old and a bachelor. He was impressive looking, with his thinning brown hair and rich olive complexion common to people born in southern France. He had come from a wealthy family, but he had avoided the world of commerce, choosing to be a teacher and a writer.

His influence on the political life of France was enormous.

Laboulaye was a Republican whose great wit and imagination had made him a favorite lecturer in the law at the College de France. However, because of a scholarly disposition and delicate health, he had long avoided the arena of French politics.

But finally, in 1865, he was elected to the French Senate.

Prior to his election, he had attempted to reach the conscience of the French people solely through his writings. His most ambitious work was a three-volume *History of the United States*. In its prologue, he related the story of Benjamin Franklin and George Washington at the Constitutional Convention in Philadelphia. A sun had been painted on the back of Washington's presidential chair and Franklin, during the convention, had been unable to decide whether the sun was rising or setting.

Finally, at the finish of the convention, Franklin exclaimed enthusiastically, "Now, at the end, I am happy to see that it is clearly a rising sun and not a sun becoming extinct."

"Franklin was right," Laboulaye announced, "it was the dawn of a new world . . . it was Liberty that rose on the other side of the Atlantic to enlighten the universe."

The idea of America as the new world was constantly in his thoughts. To an ancient civilization parched by bloody upheavals and the lies of tyrants, it seemed to offer mankind's final hope. Although he was never to visit the United States, he was certain that the time had come—"when a bewildered France searches for its way but does not find it."—to turn to this new world.

Now, in January 1871, Senator Edouard de Laboulaye left his wooded estate at Glatigny and headed toward the heart of Paris. Hysterical mobs were already setting fire to the city. There were constant rumors that the war casualties were enormous, far in excess of those which the War Office had been allowed to publish.

The Prussians had moved into the south of France and across the northeast, pillaging and raping the inhabitants of the cities that they conquered. At Sedan, Napoleon III had been captured. Although they were encountering fierce guerrilla opposition, Bismarck's troops were pressing forward to descend upon the French capital.

The military defeat of the French army was not only humiliating, it had created such panic that every Frenchman now feared for his life.

Senator Laboulaye's carriage moved quietly along the Champs Elysees, jammed with frightened crowds awaiting the inevitable. He could still envision that same boulevard forty years before . . . and a solitary figure on a white horse.

On a spring morning in 1830, a youth of nineteen watched George Washington's most famous lieutenant ride up the Champs Elysées in a ceremony honoring him as the great hero of France and America. Still a resplendent figure in his blue and white uniform, the Marquis de Lafayette was seventy-three.

Once, like the young man, Lafayette had been nineteen. At that age, overwhelmed by prospects of glory, he had traveled to America to fight for the freedoms man had dreamed of for centuries—constitutional law—representative government—free press—free speech. He had succeeded in helping to found a new nation such as the world had never known—only to return to his own country to watch Liberty swept away. What a mockery it must have been for Lafayette to have served George Washington, and then to hear his countrymen praise Napoleon as the greatest of revolutionary heroes.

On that spring morning in 1830, as Lafayette's white charger trotted along the flagstones northward toward the Arc de Triomphe, the young man watched the old soldier with sadness. During the French Revolution, Lafayette had been imprisoned, until in 1798 he was freed by the victorious Napoleon Bonaparte, who suddenly announced, "Lafayette alone in France holds fast to the original idea of Liberty."

It was an odd accolade coming from a dictator who would soon attempt to seize control of Europe.

Laboulaye loved the United States. In the years that followed, he openly professed the principles that Lafayette had fought for. He taught them in his classes at the College de France where, after de Tocqueville's death in 1859, he took on the role as the leading French authority on American constitutional history.

During the American Civil War, Laboulaye had spoken out against slavery and, in 1862, in a widely circulated article, when the success of the Union was still in doubt, he did not hesitate to point out to his countrymen which side they must support:

> Frenchmen, who have not forgotten Lafayette nor the glorious memories he left behind in the new world—it is your cause which is on trial in the United States . . . This cause has been defended by energetic men for a year with equal courage and ability; our duty is to range ourselves around them, and to hold aloft with a firm hand that old French banner, on which is inscribed, Liberty.

Since his first glimpse of Lafayette that spring morning, forty years before on the Champs Elysées, Laboulaye had longed for the day when France would be a Republic, free at last from the mercenary suppression of dictators and commissioners.

It was January 1871. Senator Laboulaye's carriage passed the site where Louis XVI had been beheaded. It crossed the Pont de la Concorde, and continued along the bank of the Seine into the Boulevard St. Germain for half a mile.

Finally, his coachman turned east up rue de Tournon.

In the distance, Edouard de Laboulaye could see the black cupola at the end of the street still flying the blue, white, and red tricolor which Lafayette had given to France.

His carriage drove through the great entranceway, emblazoned with the words *Liberté, Egalité, Fraternité,* and clattered across the yellow and chalk-grey tiled courtyard facing the fountains of the Luxembourg Gardens, which stretched as far as the eye could see.

Laboulaye climbed down from the carriage and entered the palace building, which had once been a gift from Cardinal Richelieu to Catherine de Medici. From the broad marble hallways smelling of rich wood, he slowly ascended the stairway to the enormous council room, with its long nave and sixty-foot ceiling, its gold gilt walls shimmering beneath massive crystal chandeliers.

Along dark parquet floors, beneath heroic statues and paintings, past balconies that looked out over the courtyard below, he walked through the mirrored doors into the main Senate chamber.

Three hundred senators sat in red velvet chairs.

The fate of France would be decided in that room. The thousands of tiny faces carved into the chamber's cherry-wood paneling appeared to watch silently, intently.

Laboulaye climbed the stairs to the front platform and stood alone at the lacquered inlaid lectern. With his black frock coat buttoned close to his chin and his gentle, low-pitched voice, he seemed more like a scholar than a politician. Yet he was no longer addressing a class at the College de France. There would be resistance in that room to everything he was about to say. The corrupt, self-serving friends of the emperor would challenge any attempt to form a Republic. They had profited too greatly from those years which had led to this awful moment of France's humiliation. They would not step aside without a struggle.

Laboulaye began to speak, not with impassioned rhetoric, but with the thoughtfulness of a man who believed every word:

> Liberty represents the individual life . . . the State represents the common interest of society. The two can exist side by side . . . but never should they become one . . . so that the individual is sacrificed to the State.

Despite the inspiring pleas of Senator Edouard de Laboulaye, the Senate firmly rejected his motion to form a Republic. The matter was now in the hands of the National Assembly, which was convened in Bordeaux. Garibaldi was selected as a delegate from Dijon.

With his followers disintegrating all around him, Garibaldi was surprised at his summons by the architects of the new government. Though the Royalists had immediately claimed that, as an alien, he was ineligible to serve, the Radicals in turn insisted that he had every right because he had been born in the French town of Nice.

Garibaldi asked Auguste to accompany him to Bordeaux. On that day, excited crowds overflowed the streets and cheered as the two men approached the building where the National Assembly was to meet. But as Garibaldi entered the chambers, dressed in his usual red shirt, poncho, and kepi, the Royalists gave him a hostile reception. When they demanded that he remove his military cap, he refused, saying that it was as proper for him to wear it as it was for the priests present to wear their black velvet skull caps.

As Garibaldi was called upon to speak, there was shouting everywhere, fights broke out among the delegates. At last, order was achieved, and Garibaldi stood up. In a weary voice, he stated that he was rendering his last service to France. He had come there, he had fought for them, because he wished for the French people to share the experience of Liberty. He announced that he was casting his vote in the Assembly for a Republic, and was herewith resigning his seat as a deputy.

There was chaos as the white-haired old man, accompanied by Bartholdi, began to limp from the chambers. The Royalists shouted that he could not resign because, as a foreigner, he had not validly been a member. The Radicals shouted back at them with fury.

Amidst the violent storm that followed, the old revolutionary withdrew in silent dignity as the Assembly president declared the session ended.

An armistice was signed. Napoleon III was imprisoned in Berlin.

After Garibaldi disbanded his troops at Autun, Auguste left the front lines and wandered with the long rows of retreating soldiers into Paris. What he witnessed when he entered the city overwhelmed him. People were starving. Cats were retailing at six francs a carcass, rats at one franc each, and dogmeat sold for one franc a pound.

He saw desperate men and women with nets drawing the huge yellow carp from the pool in the Luxembourg Gardens and roasting them on street corners over smudge pots. Along rue Royale and Boulevard des Capucines, young girls offered themselves for a few crusts of bread.

The city had been entirely surrounded, cut off by the thick flood of German armies, until it was finally isolated. Telegraph lines were severed and all mail service was discontinued. Bismarck had no intention of allowing the Parisians to communicate the horror of their condition to the outside world. From his head-quarters in Versailles, he demanded an indemnity of five billion francs and Alsace-Lorraine.

He was intent on starving the city until his conditions were met.

There was no one left to defend the people. The French soldiers had fought valiantly despite the perfidy of Napoleon III's com-missaires, who had so ruthlessly profiteered on war supplies that boots fell apart, cartridges neglected to explode and rifles failed to fire. It had been a terrible winter, but the French politicians, rather than quarter the troops with potential voters, ordered them to sleep on the frozen ground. The peasantry would only sell foodstuffs for double the normal price, so the defeated soldiers were soon dying of hunger and exposure.

Auguste had an apartment on rue Vavin, a studio where at the age of twenty-one he had sculpted his famous statue of General Rapp. Arriving there, he wrote in his diary:

> The Prussians are everywhere. Smoke over Paris . . . so many Prussians! Ruins at the Paris gate, horses disembow-elled . . . at the Tuilleries, Cour des Comptes, sad . . . houses in ruins, facades torn to pieces . . . poor Paris!

That evening he made his way to the home of the one man he respected more than anyone in France.

It was a comfortable, large house on a private estate beyond the Bois de Boulogne, in the middle of a rural forest known as Gla-tigny.

The figure of Edouard de Laboulaye approached.

The two men had been friends for five years, but Laboulaye had been an admirer of Bartholdi's work from the time it was first exhibited in Paris in the late 1850s. Although in age they were twenty-two years apart, both men possessed the same patriotic fervor, an uncorrupted zeal that joined them in the desire to save their country.

As they adjourned from the front veranda into Laboulaye's elegant drawing room, the famous senator admitted his feelings of depression. The Royalist politicians still had an unbreakable grip on the country. There would be no Republic. After the with-drawal of Bismarck and his army, there would probably be an-other period of dictatorship, with a new tyrant.

And once again, they talked about the gift to America.

The gift had first been discussed at a dinner party Laboulaye gave at Glatigny for a gathering of artists and intellectuals in 1865. Bartholdi had been invited as a guest of some of his patrons, and the two met for the first time. During that dinner, Laboulaye proposed a remarkable idea. They had been discussing Lafayette, when Laboulaye mused that since it was only in America that Lafayette's vision existed, perhaps, in commemoration, a sculptured gift might be presented to the people of the United States—not from the French government—but from the *people* of France.

Such a gift would not only recall the allegiance of Washington and Lafayette, but also exist as a reminder that there were those in France who still cherished Liberty. The gift would not symbolize the bloody days of Robespierre and the execution of Louis XVI, but would be a gesture of admiration for the American Declaration of Independence. Even if the French nation could not fully embrace the concept of Liberty itself and form a constitutional government of its own, it could pay homage to a nation where that experiment had so triumphantly succeeded.

Bartholdi eagerly responded to the thought of creating a monument dedicated to Liberty. But how would they raise the money?

Laboulaye was certain that there were enough Frenchmen who would back such a proposal. But they would have to work swiftly so that the gift could be completed by 1876, in time for the hundreth anniversary of American independence. They had exactly five years to raise the funds, construct the monument, and secure America's agreement to accept it.

Despite their joy over the idea, there were doubts as to the reaction of the people of the United States. Neither Laboulaye nor Bartholdi had ever even been to America. Laboulaye suggested that Bartholdi cross the ocean as soon as possible "to study it" and bring back his impressions.

When Bartholdi left Laboulaye many fears were upsetting him. He knew that the Germans occupied Colmar, and his mother was alone. But before beginning his journey home, he had one obligation that had to be looked after. It was always sad and frustrating when he visited Vanves, the tiny town just west of Paris. There, in a private house, his brother Charles had been kept for almost a decade.

Auguste found his brother unchanged. Charles was now forty-one. He spent most of his time playing with neckties and raking torn pieces of paper. At times, he would call out the name of the woman he had passionately loved for so long—Fanny Spire, whose maiden name was Dreyfus. He was attended by a valet, who tried to amuse him when he would begin crying too loudly.

Auguste was not sure that Charles even recognized him. Once Auguste had been so proud of him. Charles had been a painter with extraordinary talent. With his russet cheeks and devilish laugh, he had been colorful, alive.

Charles's tragedy was a lesson to Auguste. He would always be cautious in romance. As he confided in a letter:

> If I ever meet a person who could make me believe in the possibility of true happiness, I would let myself be drawn in, but to think of marriage, to make a decision of that kind and to look for someone, to make the best of it, never.

5

Colmar

AUGUSTE WAS an exile in Colmar. The gracious, four-story Bartholdi house, on rue des Marchands, with its rooms of oil paintings and fine Louis XIV and Louis XV furniture, was occupied by the German army. Charlotte Bartholdi was relegated to a few rooms on the fourth floor. Although they were officially in command, the Germans had learned to avoid Charlotte's piercing black looks and her sharp tongue. They were a constant nuisance to her, tramping up and down the narrow wooden stairways, washing their underwear in the river and hanging it in her rose garden to dry.

Colmar was now part of a foreign country. The official spoken language was German. Hundreds of people had left their dwellings, selling them for whatever they could, rather than live under German rule.

Charlotte Bartholdi did not give up her home. The sixty-nine-year-old widow was too proud to become a refugee. Her family's holdings consisted of substantial farmlands in the surrounding countryside—vineyards, gardens, fields for raising livestock. She was accustomed to living well from her income, and she was not willing to relinquish both her status and her standard of living.

In addition to her hope that one day France would recover its lost territory, that life would return to what it had been, there was a sentimental reason for her refusal to leave Colmar. Her son Auguste's magnificent statue of General Rapp still stood in the town square.

In the first week of March 1871, when Auguste arrived, he spoke to his mother of his plan to travel to America. He described his dinner with Laboulaye and the senator's plan to promote the building of a monument commemorating America's independence. But as they spent the next few days together, and he saw how Charlotte was living, Auguste suddenly canceled his trip. The German occupation enraged him. But he knew he could not leave his mother to cope by herself.

But Charlotte insisted that he leave at once. What could he do in Alsace? The plan for a monument was far more important than her isolated life in Colmar.

Auguste packed his belongings and started on his journey. He would not be alone, he assured her; his friend, Simon, the son of a wealthy banker, had agreed to travel with him to America.

Leaving Colmar, Auguste journeyed across France to the seaport of Brest. Laboulaye had forwarded to him a packet containing a passport and letters of recommendation to friends in the United States. The packet also contained Laboulaye's formal instructions:

> Propose to our friends over there to make with us a monument, a common work, in remembrance of the ancient friendship of France and the United States. We will take up a subscription in France. If you find a happy idea, a plan that will excite public enthusiasm, we are convinced that it will be successful on both continents, and we will do a work that will have a far-reaching moral effect.

From Brest, Auguste telegraphed Laboulaye:

> I will try to glorify the Republic and Liberty over there, in the hope that someday I will find it again here.

America

You make me weep, you with your enthusiasm for the
Republic . . . how can you go on believing in such fantasies?
—GEORGE SAND to Flaubert, 1871

Lafayette came over at Fulton Street in a large canary-colored
open barouche, drawn by four magnificent white horses. He had
consented to lay the cornerstone with his own hands. Some half
a mile over from the ferry, he stopt, got out of the barouche, and
in the midst of a crowd, with other gentlemen, assisted in lifting
the children, amid the deep-cut excavations and heaps of stones,
to safe spots where they could see the ceremony. Happy to stand
by, I remember I was taken up by Lafayette in his arms and held
a moment—I remember that he press'd my cheek with a kiss as
he set me down—I recall my feelings—the childish wonder and
nonchalance during the whole affair at the time—contrasting
with the indescribable preciousness of the reminiscence since.
—WALT WHITMAN, from an un-
published recollection of his
childhood in Brooklyn

BARTHOLDI WAS becoming restless. He had been at sea for ten
days. By noon of June 17, 1871, aboard the French steamship
Pereire, position forty-two degrees latitude, fifty-one degrees lon-
gitude, he wrote to his mother:

> We are now opposite the banks of Newfoundland; but for
> all that, there is nothing to see . . . for a whole week one
> might suppose that the world was created for fish rather
> than mankind. . . .

The picture that emerges is that of an earnest, inexperienced traveler. One concern was his inability to speak and understand English. He practiced by day on the American passengers on board. At night he walked the deck mumbling the phrases he had learned, repeating the words like a priest reciting his breviary.

He was heading toward the new world.

The industrialization of America was breathtaking. In twenty years, railroad lines throughout the country had increased from 7,475 to 62,647 miles. Businessmen who built textile factories along the rivers of the northeast made millions. President Ulysses S. Grant, in his address to the Forty-first Congress, predicted:

> There is no reason why we should not advance in material
> prosperity and happiness as no other nation ever did.

The economic miracle was symbolized by Cornelius Vanderbilt, the richest man in the country, who had lifted himself to the heights of commercial splendor by his own bootstraps. Others followed, striking it rich in oil, copper, and silver, while people everywhere were invigorated by the rough freedom of frontier life, which poet Joaquin Miller described in his book *Songs of the Sierras:*

> *Room! Room to turn around in, to breathe*
> *and be free*
> *And to grow to be giant . . .*
> *My plains of Americas! Seas of wild lands!*

Early on the fourteenth day of the voyage, Auguste scanned the misty horizon for a lighthouse or a glimpse of land. He had been on deck since 3 A.M.

> The sky grew pink—a multitude of little sails seemed to
> skim the water—our fellow travelers pointed out a cloud
> of smoke at the farther end of the bay—it was New York!

The sun rose until the daylight was strong enough for Auguste to see grass and fields of grain. As the ship sailed into New York harbor, he envisioned what he had longed for:

> At the view of the harbor of New York, the definite plan was first clear to my eyes.

Reaching for his drawing pad, he swiftly sketched what he saw—in the background, Manhattan extended to a misty horizon—the Hudson River and a corner of New Jersey appeared on the left—the unfinished towers of the Brooklyn Bridge spanned the East River to the right.

Rapidly he drew his vision.

In the center of the harbor, rising into a bright sky, he sketched a colossus—a giant bronze woman—a statue of immense proportions, whose height surpassed the Virgin of Puy, the Colossus of Rhodes, the towers of Notre Dame Cathedral. The Statue was a goddess protecting a shelter, a haven, a home.

Long afterward he recalled the moment, and how "the Statue was born for his place, which inspired its conception."

Landing on the West Side at pier 52, he found Manhattan to be almost "Chinese"—

> The city has a strange appearance. You find yourself forthwith in the midst of a confusion of railroad baggage cars, omnibuses, heavily laden drays, delicate vehicles with wheels like circular spiderwebs, the sound of hurrying crowds, neglected cobbled streets, the pavement scarred with railroad tracks, roadways out of repair, telegraph poles on each side of the street, lamp-posts not uniform, signs, wires, halliards of flags hanging across the streets, open fronts of stores such as one sees at a fair, broken down sidewalks encumbered with merchandise. . . .

Beyond, Auguste discovered that the principal avenues were well cared for, but it was the short sidestreets that fascinated him with their

> eight-storey or two storey buildings and shacks—all together, pell-mell. There are forgotten and neglected trees—some of them seem to have their roots in the cellars.

With his friend Simon, the banker's son who had accompanied him from France, Auguste found lodgings in a rooming house located at 619 Broadway, near Houston Street.

That first night, he was unable to sleep, thinking about the colossal Statue he had envisioned.

The following morning he again took a ferryboat across New York harbor. He observed that within the harbor there were three islands. The two largest were Governors and Ellis Islands. The smallest, which Auguste mentally chose for his monument, was called Bedloe's Island. In his diary dated June 22 he wrote:

> Went to Staten Island by ferryboat to study the roadstead.
> The little island seems to me the best site.

That week in Manhattan, he met with Horace Greeley, editor of the *New York Tribune,* and William George Curtis, publisher of *Harper's Weekly.* Neither Greeley nor Curtis was willing to publicize the project. He then discussed his plan for the Statue with two of New York's richest men, Cyrus Field, who had put a cable under the Atlantic, and the manufacturer Peter Cooper. Both men told him they could see no commercial prospects in such a venture.

Auguste was filled with trepidation.

No one seemed interested in a Statue that the people of France wished to present to the people of the United States. As an artist, he was in need of a commission to work on. Auguste began to consider alternatives:

> The greatest difficulty, I believe, will be with the American character, which is hardly open to things of the imagination . . . I believe that the realization of my project will be a matter of luck. I do not intend to attach myself to the project absolutely if its realization is too difficult. . . . We shall see what happens. . . . The important thing is to find a few people who have a little enthusiasm for something other than themselves and the Almighty Dollar. For that, I must meet a considerable number of people; and then, if my project is impossible of realization, I shall have made enough acquaintances here so that American amateurs of art will come to see me in Paris, and some of them will take it into their heads to ask me for my sculptures.

It was not that Auguste doubted his plan for the great Statue, but the thought of such an ambitious project and of having to propose the idea for the first time to a nation of strangers on foreign soil, presented a trying, if not impossible task.

Auguste Bartholdi explored his new surroundings. He made a visit to Central Park, which became his favorite place in Manhattan:

> Its name proves that the Americans anticipate being surrounded, soon, by the city.

He observed that Central Park resembled the Bois de Boulogne in Paris. There he found a meteorological laboratory

> in charge of a Mr. Draper, who, by means of many ingenious instruments, obtains a record on paper of all the variations of the thermometer, the hygrometer, and the wind. The park—which is the same type as the Bois de Boulogne in Paris—is admirably laid out. The area contains rocks and ponds which lend themselves very well to the design. It is very cheerful, elegant, well cared for and clean. It is the pet and pride of the city.

Ever the critical artist, he commented further:

> Here and there are some rather mediocre statues . . . .

On June 25, Auguste recorded impressions of his first Sunday in New York City in his diary:

> Not the least sound of vehicles in the Not the least sound of vehicles in the streets— nothing —people walk differently today from week days—men wearing diamonds.

Henri Maillard, owner of the New York City rooming house where Auguste and Simon stayed, invited them to Sunday dinner at his country home on the Harlem River.

The following Saturday, Auguste left New York. He traveled by steamer to Long Branch, New Jersey, to meet friends of Laboulaye. To counter the rebuff in New York, his plan was to continue on to Philadelphia and Washington, D.C., and reach out for support from other sources.

He delighted in the pleasures of a unique American excursion steamer:

> On the ground floor—the restaurant, the service, the baggage and vehicles with their horses. Richly decorated staircases lead to the floor above, where there are two great concert saloons, brilliantly decorated. In each saloon are statues, gilded decorations, and an orchestra. The song of birds fills the air—there are a hundred cages with canaries. The saloons were filled with people . . . I wanted particularly to see the bay of New York so I stayed outside on the upper deck. The orchestras had begun to play, the engine rumbled, and we started.

He and Simon checked in at Mansion House on the beach when they arrived in New Jersey.

> Four dollars a day covers the cost of lodging and board. You are supposed to eat four times a day, at certain hours, everything that is on the bill of fare.

Auguste was especially amused by the family style dining room:

> You are taken over by a waiter who brings you an enormous amount of badly cooked food in separate little dishes. Everything is big in these hotels, even the *petis pois*.

Auguste enjoyed the white sand and the warm sea air. He plunged into the cold, tingling Atlantic surf. The tranquillity of this change of scenery caused him to refocus his approach. He was, moreover, well received by the people to whom he had letters of introduction and, encouraged, he spent his time studying the American mind, the way things were done, and how he would work out his plans:

> As for my grand project, I was forced to the conclusion that I must not insist upon trying to make it take root immediately. Its realization is sure to be a long and labo-

rious process. I shall therefore take up the second part of
my program; I must move about, travel, see as many people
as possible . . . perhaps, at last, the main project will be
realized.

After two days in Long Branch, Auguste and his friend Simon
continued by train through Philadelphia and Baltimore, arriving
in Washington, D.C., on the Fourth of July. American independence was ninety-five years old, and Auguste expected a grand
celebration in the nation's capital. He was surprised to find that
there were no official ceremonies, except the constant setting off
of all sorts of explosives. He commented dryly:

This is done as much as possible under the feet of people
walking in the streets.

Washington reminded him of Versailles, with the Capitol like
a sort of Pantheon occupying the center, and everything radiating
from it. Although he found the building's architectural detail of
"only mediocre interest," he discovered its effect to be "very beautiful from a distance."

In contrast, he praised the Treasury building's great Corinthian
style. He also spent hours in the patent office studying hundreds
of models of inventions, from the steam engine to the shirt collar.

Despite the relentless summer heat, the dust and the flies, Auguste found Washington pleasing and sympathetic. Because of
Senator Laboulaye's renown, an instant introduction, he met one
of France's greatest supporters, Senator Charles Sumner of Massachusetts.

Sumner, a tall, white-haired man in his sixties, had been a vigorous antislavery leader. A famed orator, his vitriolic attacks on
Senator Andrew P. Butler of South Carolina had so incited the
latter's nephew, Representative Preston Brooks, that he tried to
kill him on the Senate floor. While Sumner was at his desk, Brooks
had caned him in fury.

Sumner was seriously injured, but he returned to deliver his
most famous "Barbarism of Slavery" speech, condemning slavery
on moral, economic and social grounds.

While serving as chairman of the Foreign Relations Committee,
Sumner had traveled to Paris, where he and Edouard de Labou-

laye became close friends. Laboulaye had written to him praising
Auguste and outlining the challenging project they had in mind.
Auguste described Sumner in his diary on July 5:

> Keen, intelligent man—loves France—seems sympathetic
> to my project.

After dining at Sumner's home, Auguste was taken by the senator on a tour of Washington. Reminded of his own country,
which lay devastated by the armies of Germany, Auguste was
especially moved by one sight:

> He showed me something curious and sad—one of the
> national cemeteries. The United States has acquired tracts
> in different parts of the country, containing the graves of
> Union soldiers, who fell in the War of the Secession. Not
> far from Washington, the government has taken over the
> beautiful property of General Lee, and has buried there
> 30,000 soldiers. Each has his headstone. The cemetery is
> vast. One sees the rows of white stones under the trees,
> extending into the distance as far as the eye can reach.
> Only too clearly, one sees the fruits of war.

On Sunday, July 9, Auguste traveled by steamboat down the
Potomac River. After two hours, the boat pulled onto the right
bank near a little wooded slope, bordered by trees dipping the
tips of their branches into the water:

> We climbed up a shady road and came to Washington's
> tomb, a small structure of brick. Looking through the door-
> way, we saw the sarcophagus. The sight of this tomb, after
> the deep impressions I have received from the spectacle of
> this great country, filled me with emotion.

Inside Washington's house, Auguste saw the key to the Bastille,
which Lafayette had presented to Washington, and the room in
which Lafayette slept when he visited Mt. Vernon. From the
porch, Auguste looked out over the Potomac and the surrounding
countryside. He had begun to sketch the river, trees, and sky when
the steamboat whistle summoned him. He rejoined the other passengers and boarded the vessel for the trip back to Washington.

That evening Auguste discussed his Statue with Senator Sumner. Sumner advised him to return in the fall when Congress was in session. There, the plan could be presented and acted upon.

The next day, Auguste went to Philadelphia. On July 11, he jotted in his diary:

> We go to dinner at the Union League Club with Lafayette's granddaughter, Mme. de Chambrun, and Charles W. Eliot, President of Harvard. I propose a toast on behalf of M. Laboulaye to our American friends.

His host in Philadelphia, Michael Forney, editor of the *Philadelphia Press,* invited him to meet a crowd of wealthy New Englanders:

> I had to tell them about Garibaldi and the war . . . Mr. Forney insists on my showing the sketches of my project. He explains them. The audience looks at them with glacial interest. I pack up and leave as quickly as possible. How much pain and exasperation must be experienced to realize a thing that, if it succeeds, will make the same people enthusiastic?

But, there were others in Philadelphia who were excited about the statue—a Mr. Orne, the city's leading merchant, and the Park Commissioner. Auguste noted:

> This pleases me, because my first days after reaching America were not so pleasant as this stage of my journey, and I was anxious about my undertaking.

Not that he was feeling less anxious about it, especially since his next meeting was with the most influential man in America—the one person who, if he wished, could do more than anyone else to secure the desired site in New York harbor—

> I went to see President Grant, who received me very kindly. I found the sovereign of the United States installed in a most simple cottage . . . The whole establishment is near the ocean—passing vessels fire salutes and dip their colors.

> The President led me to the terrace. . . . He is a cold man,
> like most Americans. . . . He displays an affability that is
> reserved and simple, but at the same time genuine. There
> is no formality. . . . I show him my project. He likes it very
> much, thinks that securing the site will not be a difficult
> problem, that the project will be submitted to Congress.
> He offers me a cigar.

On his return to New York City, Auguste was irresistibly drawn
back to the tiny island which he had chosen for his monument.
Although it was ideally located for his purpose, a military fort was
built upon it, so that there could be a possible conflict with the
army:

> I believe this difficulty will be resolved when a decision has
> been reached about the monument itself. That is the ques-
> tion. I believe this enterprise will take on very great pro-
> portions. If things turn out as I hope they will, this work
> of sculpture will become of very great moral importance.

Auguste's meetings with Senator Sumner and President Grant
had given him renewed hope for his project. While pondering his
next step, he received a letter from Charlotte Bartholdi. She was
restless and concerned:

> Dear Auguste—
> I understand how irresistible all the claims of power are
> across such enormous distances. I read and reread the ar-
> ticle I have about New York, and my mind follows you and
> tries to picture every place where my dear Auguste perhaps
> finds himself. . . .
> By winter the farm will be in better condition . . . I am
> ready to rent the ground floor by creating an exit between
> the casement windows, but this will not be ready until St.
> Michael's day. I hope by then these Prussians will have
> gotten out.

She confessed to her continuing feud with a German army
officer billeted in her home:

> I have brought down the officer to the small dining room.

On my order, I have made [the hired man] throw papers around and make the room dusty so this officer will be uncomfortable and want to leave.

She ended the letter with a note to Auguste's traveling companion, whose family acted as bankers for the Bartholdis in Paris. The note, cleverly composed as a passionate prayer, was handwritten, three times on two sheets, in Latin, German, and English. Her hand, crossed-out, and reworked, looked undecipherable, but to Auguste it was quite clear. The letter asked Auguste to read the prayer to Simon:

Simones, take great care in account of my dear Augustus,
Repeat, take great, great care of my dear named Auguste.

Her rendering of the German, "O Simon, who art responsible for my Augustus, committed to thy care," to the English, "take great care in account of my dear Augustus," would seem to the German censors to be a type of simple, ignorant English—at least that is what she intended. Beneath her notations, Charlotte carefully added the figures:

25
800
0,000

It was a coded message to Simon to disburse money to Auguste should he need it. The Germans, who had forbidden financial transactions between Alsace and the rest of France, were to be kept in the dark at all costs. There was a secret Bartholdi franc account in Paris.

Immediately, by return post, Auguste responded to her message:

Do not worry about money. I have all I need. When I am at the end of my funds, I shall start for home.

From New York, Auguste took the train to Boston. He was amused by the outlandish female clothing worn in the city of patricians:

Nowhere are there bigger hoopskirts or larger chignons than in the Puritan City.

On August 2, he traveled to a cottage in nearby Nahant where he met the famed poet, Henry Wadsworth Longfellow:

> He in person received me. He has a face somewhat like Garibaldi. He showed me the greatest cordiality and much enthusiasm for my project. He insisted on my staying for dinner; and afterward we sat smoking cigars on the terrace and watching the sun set beyond the little islands in the sea.

Longfellow told him that he hoped the idea of the great Statue on Bedloe's Island would arouse enthusiasm among New Yorkers. But from his tone there was the implication that such enthusiasm might be difficult to inspire. As they parted, the elderly gentleman clasped Auguste's hand. Auguste later commented he felt as if, through the pressure of the poet's hands, he were transmitting his love to his poor, embattled friends in France.

There was little more to do in the East. It would be over a month before Congress returned to session.

Beyond lay the mountains and prairies of America. How would the inhabitants of those vast forests and plains view his grand colossus of Liberty?

Seeking further acceptance for the work he envisioned, Auguste set out, alone, toward the Pacific.

CHAPTER

3

Auguste's Diary of the West

*When—after some days of voyaging—in the pearly radiance of
a beautiful morning is revealed the magnificent spectacle of
those immense cities, of those rivers extending as far as the eye
can reach . . . when one awakens in the midst of that interior
sea covered with vessels . . . which swarms about puffing,
whistling, swinging the great arms of their uncovered walking
beams, moving to and fro like a crowd upon a public square, it
is thrilling. It is indeed the New World which appears in its
majestic expanse with the ardor of its glowing life.*
        —AUGUSTE BARTHOLDI

THE EASTERN United States with its tree-lined rivers, its industry,
and its continuous streams of people traveling from city to suburb
to town, still possessed a cramped uniformity similar to France.
But when his eyes turned west, Auguste Bartholdi became eu-
phoric over the thousands of square miles which sprawled westward into the horizon. He kept a meticulous journal of what he
saw—a prospering, young country in the summer of 1871.
    But first he traveled to Chicago, from New York and Niagara
Falls down the shores of the Great Lakes:

In 1804, five people lived here; today there are 299,000
. . . the whistles of the locomotives and steamers make a

39

continuous sound like that of an aeolian harp, smoke blackens the city; a vast population rushes about.

Chicago seemed to Bartholdi to be the most American of all cities, its population "prey to the stomach ache of business."

> The most interesting thing about Chicago is the aspect of the city itself—its works, its formation . . . for example, two tunnels under the river, and another tunnel under the bed of the lake extending 3000 metres from the shore, for the purpose of bringing pure water into the city for the use of the people . . . these things are of the greatest interest from the viewpoint of activity, ingenuity and courage. What is lacking in the city and in most of the men is charm and taste.

In Chicago he talked about his Statue to whoever would listen. He met with the Civil War hero, General Philip H. Sheridan, and with William Ogden, the great builder of railroads in the West, for whom a city in Utah had been named. Auguste's idea was to find distinguished people who would support his plan. As he wrote to his mother, he intended to form a network of these people across America:

> Do not be astonished if I go to San Francisco—it will be useful . . . Thus I shall have some personal relations in each city.

Departing Chicago by a train that cut through the heart of America, he was fascinated by the sleeping cars:

> Going to bed and getting up are amusing experiences. The corridor between the beds is narrow. Dressing and undressing is accomplished in bed, behind curtains, a difficult gymnastic exercise—rather difficult for the ladies, who nevertheless do very well. As they wear mountains of false hair in America, they simply take it off at night and the coiffures are in perfect order in the morning.

Westward the train moved on, over the Missouri River, through

Omaha and into the vast, unsettled wilderness. Auguste presented a vivid description of his experience:

> The prairies get to be monotonous after you have traveled across them for thirty-six hours. In spite of that, there is a certain charm about this immense, ocean-like expanse. From time to time there is something unexpected—a herd of antelope or a city of prairie dogs . . . I also saw, one night on the horizon, a great prairie fire . . . I have seen on the plains the skeletons of old hoop-skirts, symbols of progress—which are evidence similar to the skeletons of cattle often seen along the old emigrant trail. This ancient road is frequently visible, marked only by a few dusty furrows; it is like a prolonged foot-path, a track painfully worn in the earth by innumerable emigrants who, for month after month, dragged themselves over these endless spaces in order to cross the vast continent.

And then, suddenly, he was into the Rocky Mountains as the feeling of flatness gave way to jarring cliffs and swerving drops—

> In some places the scene is diabolical—something out of a fairy tale. We begin to cross plateaus which are 8,000 feet above sea level. Soon horizons of billowing mountains are visible. Then the road plunges into valleys and gorges. We go from one ravine to another through deep cuts, with occasional tunnels. On either side of us are masses of enormous rocks. The views are magnificent.

On August 20, Auguste entered a verdant, cultivated valley, where rested the Mormon capital, Salt Lake City. Leaving the train, he was amazed to see fine carriages in the dusty, caved-in streets, and women, elaborately and smartly dressed, walking in the company of filthy miners.

There he met the seventy-year-old Mormon leader, Brigham Young—

> He had just returned from a journey and was tired, and asked me to come back next morning and spend a few minutes with him. He is an extraordinary personage, very intelligent and full of energy; he is also very shrewd and

knows how to take advantage of human stupidity. His face
explains his character.

That evening, a commanding officer of French origin, General
Trobiand, to whom Auguste had a letter of introduction, took
him to the theater. In a proscenium box sat one of Young's sons
and two of his wives. General de Trobiand whispered to him that
Brigham Young had sixteen wives and forty-nine children.

Auguste had planned to stay only one day and a night, but he
was forced to remain an extra day. A committee of Mormons
wanted him to sculpt a bust of their leader. He was reluctant, as
the days were passing and he was anxious to get to San Francisco.
But finally, he consented—

> In the morning I went to make a sketch of the profile of
> Brigham Young for the bust that he wants me to model.
> He told me that he hadn't time and asked me to come back
> the next day. I told him, politely, to go about his business.

Packing his belongings, Auguste again boarded a train westward:

> At Ogden we take the great, transcontinental line. Leaving
> at five in the evening, we see in the distance the Great Salt
> Lake and a very beautiful sunset behind the mountains. A
> few little fires scattered along the dark plain show where
> Indians are encamped. The darkness swallows up their
> shadowy forms. All next day we cross rugged and savage
> country. . . . The landscape is uneven—the railroad tracks,
> unable to find a level bed, must climb and descend. The
> whole area is a desert. . . . We reach the passages of the
> high mountains of Nevada. . . . Mining settlements, dev-
> astated forests, the tortured earth, a few scattered little
> houses of wood . . . vast silhouettes of mountains, deep
> valleys, scrap iron and broken lumber. . . . Near the in-
> habited places the landscape seems to have been hastily
> torn up and scattered by man in his furious search for gold.
> All this seems like a battlefield.

The train stopped at Horn Gap, California, and then began its
descent from mountain to mountain, toward the rich, cultivated

land of the Sacramento Valley, an enormously productive area, abundant with magnificent oranges, cherries, grapes, plums, pears, peaches, and apricots.

Another hundred miles and they were at the entrance to San Francisco Bay—

> I am very glad to have come here, for the place is most extraordinary. It is really a very good thing to see the world in its various aspects, to encounter customs and ideas from an outside viewpoint. I sometimes have the feeling that I am observing our globe hanging in the immensity of space. Human affairs seem so small. . . .

Following the gold rush of the 1850s and 1860s, San Francisco had become a boom town of tents and wooden shacks. On top of Nob Hill and Telegraph Hill, ornate mansions were being constructed, while beneath them, along Pacific Street, Kearny, and Grant Avenue, all-night gambling parlors, saloons, and palatial bordellos flourished.

Auguste had never witnessed anything like the tough, sprawling city, teeming with overnight millionaires, raucous dance halls, and the thousands of prostitutes who inhabited the notorious Barbary Coast—

> At San Francisco, I believe people are more materialistic than anywhere else; and I believe that temporarily the population has not been educated on a very high moral plane. Men of greedy ambition are attracted hither—there is hardly room for anything else. . . . In contrast with most American cities, San Francisco is exceedingly bumpy and hilly, except the part close to the water. Most of the streets are paved with wooden planks. The houses are almost all of wood. . . . The city ends nowhere; it loses itself in the hills and in the sand of highways under construction, along which are isolated, out-of-repair wooden shacks like those of an abandoned carnival.

His campaign for his Statue was directed at the city's civic leaders—Leland Stanford, James Phelan, Collis Potter Huntington—but there is little evidence that he got anywhere beyond publicizing the project to whoever would listen. Finally, he settled down to enjoy the myriad picturesque sights, strolling the streets of the town, which he found crowded and exciting—

> There are not a few theaters here, and some of them far surpass the most risqué theaters of Paris. Yesterday I went with a number of Frenchmen to a Chinese theater, a real Chinese theater. It was horribly funny—music that would make your hair stand on end, fantastic yapping and meowing, extravagant costumes and make-up . . . the effect was beautiful in color. We were surrounded by Chinese whose pig-tails hung over the backs of the benches where they were seated. All the time we were there we felt like scratching ourselves. I had the satisfaction, however, of leaving the theater without having taken anything away from my neighbors.

Already Bartholdi was planning his return to the East. He decided to bypass the Yosemite Valley where he felt there was too much to experience in the time remaining. But he did make one side trip to see the thousand-year-old giant redwoods that soared three hundred feet into the sky—

> A whole day's trip by stagecoach—and what a stagecoach, and what roads, and what dust! Imagine a road like the dry bed of one of our mountain cascades, paved with a layer of dust that made it look smooth. I had to hunch over and climb on all fours. When I stopped to rest, the dust poured from my hat like sand in an hourglass . . . We arrived by night at a sort of hotel—like the Hohwald—in the depths of the forest. First of all, one must pull himself together, for the walk is enough to take away anyone's breath. After supper I left the house and strolled around in the moonlight. I saw some of the Big Trees, these colossi, here and there among trees of ordinary size. But the ordinary trees themselves are so big that the arms of two men can scarcely encompass them. The impression we get in the midst of this forest is truly amazing; and you wonder what effect this spectacle had on the first man who, without warning, came upon it.

To his fellow travelers Auguste must have been an amusing

sight, a cultured Frenchman, covered continually with a layer of dust, wide-eyed, dazed by the extremities of the wild west. Once more he boarded the rickety old stagecoach, heading south—

> ...we reached the mining country at Murphy and Los Angeles ... I wanted only to get a glimpse of this part of the country; I saw the principal sights, the general aspect, the mines, the forest, and some wild, rugged scenes. Los Angeles is a mining town, with stamp mills, streams, as well as excavacations everywhere. I confined myself to a glimpse of the surface of things ... the road is of little interest—farms, cultivated land, dried-up fields, arid and dusty land ... I took the train for Stockton, where the hotel boy promptly dusted me off with a feather duster.

He had decided to take a different route home, through the mountains of Nevada into Wyoming, switching to the railroad line that ran south to Denver, Kansas City, and St. Louis. More than ever, the romantic solitude of his journey invaded the rhythm of his thoughts—

> At Cheyenne the prairie begins—the endless prairie, rolling, undulating, with little dried-up ravines, rocks and stony hills. But it is all like a desert—no trees and a faraway horizon. . . . You gaze upon it as upon the ocean; the undulating land and the depressions follow one another like ground swells. At this season, the colors resemble those of a cashmere shawl—broad, black surfaces often appear especially near the railroad, for the sparks from the locomotive frequently cause great fires in the dry grass, which grows bright green again in the following year.

He passed clusters of buffalo, which became more frequent—

> I saw in the distance a herd of about a thousand. Some of them near the railroad ran away. One, standing on a knoll and watching us pass, looked like a huge, black-maned lion.

Traveling through eastern Colorado, with its greyish terrain sparsely populated by pine trees, they crossed into seemingly endless fields of green grass, the flat farmlands of Kansas. The train passed over the Missouri River—

The Missouri—as is the case with most American rivers—seemed to glide, like a muddy inundation, level with its very low, wooded shores. The bright rays of the morning sun, mirrored in the water, melted away in purple mists towards the horizon. For some time, we passed through superb forests, to which the autumn has begun to give the most lovely tints. The bindweed and Virginia creeper, in autumnal colors, stretch from one tree to another. . . . These plants, like a band of voluptuaries, with their feet in the rich, swampy earth and their heads bathed in sunlight, seem to indulge in gestures of the wildest extravagance . . . later the land rises. More of the forest is clearer—there are farms and immense fields of corn.

Suddenly the din of St. Louis aroused him:

We can distinguish the masses of brick buildings and chimneys and hear the half-suffocated breathing of the steamers, whose lights are reflected in the waters of the river. A few moments later we leave the train amid the shouts of the runners for the hotels. An omnibus takes us across several streets, while the traffic makes way for us. A few isolated gas-jets show that there are windows and doors in the dark shapes on either side of the street. Merchandise and signs indicate that we are approaching the center of the city's life.

Following his usual procedure, Auguste met with the civic leaders of St. Louis, including State Senator Carl Shurz. Shurz owned a German newspaper, the *Westliche Post*, which employed a vigorous, young reporter, Joseph Pulitzer. Although Pulitzer and Auguste did not meet, the young reporter would play a crucial role in the story of the Statue of Liberty.

Auguste outlined his ideas for the Statue to Shurz, who was enthusiastic. Shurz gave him a tour of the city, and what impressed Auguste above everything was the St. Louis school system:

When you observe the attention given here to training and education, you understand the greatest achievements of Americans. They apply themselves in the highest degree of educational problems. It is one of the finest things about America—and the noblest.

Hurrying his return to the East, Auguste arrived in Washington on September 29—

> All my work hangs by threads. I must make all possible arrangements before leaving in order to be sure that they will not break after I have left. Mine has been a diplomatic task and I have great hopes. This voyage will probably have a profound influence on my whole career, and I am sure that good things will come of it.

He was to be disappointed.

Congress had returned to session and the project for his great Statue had been discussed. Even with the support of Senator Sumner, it was felt throughout the Capitol that the French would have to take the financial initiative before they could expect the slightest help from the United States.

Frustrated by America's response, Auguste wearily left Washington:

> I have seen a fearful number of people and begin to be a little tired of it. Surely one must be animated with the sacred fire of his art to do what I have done. Otherwise, more than once I would have dropped the whole affair. But I have faith in the outcome, and I believe that my work, beyond its artistic interest, will have a moral value that will be appreciated some day!

But when would that day come?

As he prepared for his return to France, Auguste was hard put to enumerate the benefits of his trip for his final note to his mother:

> Well, for the time being, I have not accomplished any definite result—perhaps that will come later. I should have liked to give you some pleasant news for your birthday. For want of anything better, I shall confine myself to saying . . . that I thank you for seeing America through my eyes and most especially for having given me my eyes and my ability to see with them.

He had one more visit to make, to his friends, the La Farges, in Newport, Rhode Island.

He would meet an architect and a lady.

The architect would not only share his vision of the great Statue, but one day help make it a reality.

With the lady he would fall in love.

CHAPTER

4

Jeanne-Emilie

*Of all the men who had deeply affected their friends since 1850,
John La Farge was certainly the foremost . . . La Farge alone
owned a mind complex enough to contrast against the
commonplaces of American uniformity, and in the process had
vastly perplexed most Americans who came in contact with it.*
—from *The Education of Henry Adams*

BORN AND raised in New York's Greenwich Village, John La
Farge was dashing and good-looking, with a thin face, a receding
hairline and ever-curious brown eyes. He had a distaste for shak-
ing hands. In fact, something in his nature shrank from all personal contact. La Farge was to become the grandfather of Oliver
La Farge, anthropoligist and author of the celebrated novel *Laugh-
ing Boy.*

La Farge was six feet tall, with an intense ego. He was a shy,
fastidious, aloof genius who, at thirty-six, was one of the most
famous painters in America.

The La Farge summer home on Sunnyside Place in Newport
was the haven for a group of brilliant young artists who came
together, not to discuss the buying and selling of their work, but
to explore the infinite refinements of perception and expression—what they lived for in their hearts. It was one of those rare

meeting places where an artist could feel that he was both safe and cared for. John La Farge's close friends were Henry James and James Whistler. La Farge was an uncanny observer of human nature and extremely effective at igniting those around him to pursue their true artistic bents, despite their own uncertainties. He had encouraged Henry James to become a writer rather than an artist. When the youthful Stanford White had sought him out, yearning to be a painter, La Farge had prodded him, instead, to embrace architecture.

John La Farge was Auguste Bartholdi's best friend. They had met when they were both studying art in Paris in the 1850s. As eager students, they had been constantly in the company of Gautier, Baudelaire, Flaubert, and Sainte-Beuve, forever planning great things and forever talking about them at dinners, in the corridors of theaters and all night long in their favorite Parisian cafes. Now, almost twenty years later, as the two men sat on the long porch in the afternoon sunlight in Newport, Auguste told La Farge of his lack of success in America.

La Farge strongly urged Auguste to pursue his great project. In order to help him financially, La Farge managed to obtain for Auguste a commission to build a sculptural frieze on the Romanesque tower of a Unitarian church in Boston.* It was agreed that Auguste would work on the project when he went back to Paris.

One evening, a neighbor stopped by, a young architect with a neatly trimmed reddish beard and strikingly forceful eyes.

His name was Richard Morris Hunt.

Born in Vermont, he had also studied in Paris, at the Ecole des Beaux-Arts in the 1840s. There he had gained such renown that his influential teacher, Hector Martin Lefuel, offered him any governmental position in his control if he would stay in France.

But Hunt was restless to return to America, feeling that his native land needed to be awakened to the visual arts of Europe.

Upon his return, Hunt was caught up in the world of the very rich—the Astors, the Vanderbilts, the Goelets—for whom he built luxurious palaces and chateaux.

---

*The frieze still exists on the tower of the same church, which is now the First Baptist Church in Boston. At each corner of the tower is an angel holding a trumpet. On the sides are large sculptured groups representing four events in the life of a Christian: baptism, first communion, marriage, and death. For the characters in the frieze, Auguste used the faces of some of the people he had met in America, including the poet Longfellow.

The young Auguste Bartholdi in Paris before his triumph. (COURTESY OF MUSÉE BARTHOLDI, COLMAR)

Driven by madness, Charles Bartholdi tried to kill his brother. (COURTESY OF MUSÉE BARTHOLDI, COLMAR)

Monument Voulminot in the cemetery at Colmar was Auguste Bartholdi's angry spectre of human hope. It became a symbol to the people of Alsace-Lorraine that the day would come when they would beat back the Germans and regain their liberty. Twisted by defeat, the black arm with its grotesque hand and fingers appears to creep toward a tantalizing sword just out of reach. (AUTHOR'S COLLECTION)

Bartholdi's gigantic writhing lion, seventy-two feet long and thirty-six feet high, carved out of the side of a granite cliff overlooking Belfort, was eulogized by poet Francois Coppee: *"Great Lion, Symbol of anger and rebellion, You give us the assurance of a future less dark. . ."* (AUTHOR'S COLLECTION)

Eduoard de Laboulaye fought to keep the flame of Liberty from being extinguished in France. He dreamed that it would be forever enshrined in America. (COURTESY OF CONSERVATOIRE NATIONAL DES ARTS ET METIÉRS, PARIS)

Bartholdi with his mother, Charlotte, the model for the Statue of Liberty's face. (COURTESY OF MUSÉE BARTHOLDI, COLMAR)

Bartholdi about to play the violin, his mother, seated, and Jeanne-Emilie standing beside the piano. (COURTESY OF MUSÉE BARTHOLDI, COLMAR)

Bartholdi's studio in Paris where his wife Jeanne-Emilie modeled for the Statue of Liberty. (COURTESY OF MUSÉE BARTHOLDI, COLMAR)

Bartholdi in his studio prepares to oversee construction of his Statue of Liberty. (COURTESY OF MUSÉE BARTHOLDI, COLMAR)

Over two hundred plaster parts of the body and clothing had to be formed. They were then pressed with thin copper. (COURTESY OF MUSÉE BARTHOLDI, COLMAR)

In the huge workshop of Gaget, Gauthier et Cie, the guildsmen of Les Compagnons form the wooden molds. (COURTESY OF MUSÉE BARTHOLDI, COLMAR)

The wooden framework for the hand about to be covered with plaster. (COURTESY OF MUSÉE BARTHOLDI, COLMAR)

The Statue's arm awaits the repoussé process. (COURTESY OF MUSÉE BARTHOLDI, COLMAR)

Paris, 1876. After a century of political struggle and bloodshed, the Statue finally lifted her torch of Liberty. (COURTESY OF MUSÉE BARTHOLDI, COLMAR)

In 1878, transported by a huge horsedrawn dray through the heart of Paris, the head of the Statue of Liberty was exhibited on the exact spot where Lafayette once swore the French people to a vow of allegiance. (COURTESY OF MUSÉE BARTHOLDI, COLMAR)

The brilliant Gustave Eiffel rejected the idea that the world's tallest structure should be filled with sand. Foreseeing the modern-day skyscraper, he gave the Statue a skeleton of steel. (COURTESY OF MUSÉE D'ORSAY, PARIS)

In the courtyard of Gaget, Gauthier et Cie, the Statue of Liberty comes to life over the rooftops of Paris. (COURTESY OF MUSÉE BARTHOLDI, COLMAR) ⟫⟫→

After a tragic romance, Emma Lazarus sought the heart of her people and wrote a sonnet that was unforgettable. (COURTESY OF AMERICAN JEWISH HISTORICAL SOCIETY, WALTHAM, MASSACHUSETTS)

Almost deluged by stormy seas, the warship Isère carried the pieces of Bartholdi's Statue of Liberty to America. (COURTESY OF MUSÉE BARTHOLDI, COLMAR)

Architect Richard Hunt built fantasy palaces for the very rich. But when he asked them to support the pedestal he had designed for the Statue of Liberty, they turned him down. (COURTESY OF THE METROPOLITAN MUSEUM OF ART)

Rejected by Manhattan's millionaires and scorned by the New York *Times,* the Statue of Liberty's greatest defender became fiery publisher Joseph Pulitzer. (BROWN BROTHERS)

Awaiting the unveiling of the Statue of Liberty, Bartholdi sits on an ancient gun turret on Bedloe's Island in New York. (COURTESY OF MUSÉE BARTHOLDI, COLMAR)

In temperament, Hunt and La Farge were very different. La Farge was retiring, a purist, while Hunt was outgoing, relentlessly pursuing his efforts on an awesome scale. La Farge later reminisced:

> Richard Hunt thought it useless to carry the refinement of tone and color to the extent which I aimed at in my studies, telling me that there would not be one in a hundred or five hundred artists capable of appreciating such differences of accuracy—their eye and their training would not be sufficient. So much the better, I responded, if only one man in a thousand could see it; I should then have exactly what I wanted, to appeal to the man who knew and to the mind like mine.

La Farge introduced Hunt to Auguste one evening. As they spoke, Auguste found Hunt's personality irritating. His only comment about their meeting was noted in his diary:

> Met Mr. Hunt, architect from New York, who brags a little, pleased with himself. Dined with La Farge and Madame. . . .

Ironically, there were few that Auguste had encountered since his coming to America who would prove as valuable to him as Richard Morris Hunt.

Little is known about the remainder of the evening, except for one notable event. The "Madame" Auguste referred to in his diary was John La Farge's vivacious wife, Margaret. She also had invited a lady to dinner—a Miss Jeanne-Emilie Puysieux.

Jeanne-Emilie had sharp, defined features and glowing brown eyes. There was a hesitancy to her smile, but her voice often melted with a quiet, careful laugh that was warm and affecting. She had full lips and soft, long black hair. She was not immediately beautiful, but she became adorably attractive as she spoke, her hands animating her inner feelings, her eyes dancing in the candlelight that illuminated the La Farge dining room. Her figure was delicate, but perfect. She was thirty-one. She had never been married.

When they first met, she told Auguste that she liked to be called just Jeanne. Born in France, the daughter of a wealthy clothing manufacturer who later lost his fortune, she became an orphan at the age of six.

Margaret La Farge and she were cousins and Jeanne had come to visit her with a relative from Canada, an elderly lady named Mrs. Walker. Jeanne had been raised in the town of Nancy, located several miles east of Paris, but her background was Parisian. She and Mrs. Walker had left Paris at the outbreak of the Franco-Prussian war.

Perhaps Auguste was too involved in the pursuit of his ambitions to notice that the lady could not take her eyes off him. Perhaps he barely noticed Jeanne at all as she sat quietly beside him at the La Farge table. But there is no question, as her letters reveal, that she loved him from the first moment.

His mother had written him of the difficulties in Colmar, although since her June letter there had been one change for the better:

> I have no military billeted at this moment, but anything can happen.

With a surge of gladness that he was finally coming back to her, Charlotte Bartholdi added:

> Your letter arrived on the greatest birthday of the year. It was today, 37 years ago, that a small chérubin was sent down to earth to fill my heart with joy . . . I have given thanks a thousand times for the happiness with which you have filled my existence.

America had been a difficult adventure, yet he vowed someday to return.

Auguste spent a few more days with the La Farges. In the quiet of John La Farge's studio in Newport, he constructed a primitive model of the figure he had envisioned that brief memorable moment in New York harbor. Few people knew that it was in Newport, not in Paris, that he created his first model of the Statue of Liberty.

He could picture the tiny island, the few sailing ships moving across the dark bay. Against the bright morning sky, his eternal bronze goddess rose before him, raising the burning torch of Liberty aloft in her mighty right hand—taller and grander than anything around her—so real, as if at any moment she might smile and speak, as if she were beckoning to the present, the past, to all mankind, victorious.

CHAPTER
5

The Ordeal

If glory were the same thing as fame Bartholdi would have been among the foremost of French artists. From one end of the universe to the other, in the old world and the new, his name was celebrated, his work popular, for he had the distinction of seeing on a grand scale, which is original in this age of trinkets. He had the good fortune of attaching himself to ideas and causes which passionately involved his times.

—from the French Journal *Debats,*
April 11, 1904

BARTHOLDI RETURNED from his visit to America in 1871 to find France in worse condition than before he had left. Humiliated by defeat, the country could no longer even boast of a central representative government.

A six-man committee called the *Commune* had emerged as France's sole provisional government. Though it was controlled by the Royalists, it had Leon Gambetta as a member. Gambetta was a radical Republican who had organized a guerrilla force which had continued for a while to fight against Bismarck even after a peace agreement had been reached with the Germans. Because of Gambetta's popularity, Bismarck had allowed him to come out of hiding once he had disbanded his guerrilla forces.

Without food, with their economy at a standstill, the French people were demoralized. The war had ended, but Bismarck's troops still occupied Paris, burning and plundering the city. From his headquarters within the Palace of Versailles, the German chancellor now threatened to hold the nation captive for years if his demand for an enormous ransom in retributive damages was not met.

Witnessing the desperation of his countrymen, Auguste reacted with a creative fury. In the cemetery in Colmar, side by side, were the graves of Adolphe Voulminot and Joseph Wagner, two soldiers who had died fighting alongside him at Autun. Above the two graves, Auguste designed a monument unlike any other he had created. Taking a marble slab, he made it look as if it had split apart . . . the graves seemed to have opened up . . . from the earth's depths a long, thin arm desperately groped in the light. Twisted by defeat, the black arm with its grotesque hand and fingers appeared to creep toward a tantalizing sword just out of reach.

Titled *Monument Voulminot,* it was Auguste's most dramatic sculpture. His angry specter of human hope soon became a symbol to the people in Alsace-Lorraine that the day would come when they would beat back the Germans and regain their liberty.

There was great anxiety when the *Monument Voulminot* was unveiled in the Colmar cemetery on November 2, 1872. Alsace-Lorraine was a territory now belonging to all the states of Germany and the arm Auguste had created grasping for a sword from a torn grave presented an alarming challenge.

But the Prussians, flushed with victory, were quietly tolerant. The monument was not removed.

It seemed, however, as if Auguste were still inflamed. The desire to portray man's thirst for Liberty had taken over his work.

A second artistic challenge soon presented itself.

The city of Belfort, only ten miles south of Colmar, had stubbornly fought against the Prussians, holding on for weeks. Bismarck's forces were ordered to annihilate the residents, but they refused to surrender. Because of Belfort's resistance, the French were allowed to keep the town and the land around it, although the remainder of Alsace was lost under the Treaty of Frankfurt.

In 1871, the city council of Belfort decided to commemorate

the defense of the city with a great monument and announced a contest. Auguste immediately entered the competition by submitting sketches of a huge lion to be carved on the side of a cliff.

After winning the competition, Auguste began work, but it was necessary for him to hire a crew of men for which funds had to be raised. This was accomplished when his lion was pictured in an illustrated newspaper, *Le Monde Illustre,* on May 9, 1874, and people throughout Europe were moved by Auguste's vision.

The monument took Auguste four years to build—it had to be hand carved on the side of a granite cliff overlooking Belfort. His gigantic lion was seventy-two feet long and thirty-six feet high. Wounded, writhing in pain, but still defiant, it leaned into a mass of rock, a broken spear beneath its paw, as it reared in fury at its enemies.

Shortly after Auguste finished his work in 1878, French poet François Coppée wrote:

> *Great Lion*
> *Symbol of anger and rebellion*
> *You give us the assurance of a future*
> *less dark . . .*

In 1871, Auguste had returned from his travels in the United States, hoping that money would be raised so that he could begin work on the Statue of Liberty. He had been eager to see Edouard de Laboulaye, but to his surprise, he discovered that Laboulaye had fled Paris. The Republican senator was living as a voluntary exile in the obscure village of Bolbec on the coast of Normandy.

On July 28, 1871, Laboulaye wrote explaining his circumstances to his friend John Bigelow, an official of the U.S. State Department:

> I have been threatened by men from the *Commune,* who already believe themselves certain of success and who are counting on the siege to sweep them to power. I believe it prudent to stay some distance from Paris . . . I lived in the middle of the war and the invasion. I have viewed the Prussian civilization firsthand, and I hope that the world soon awakens to the conduct of these people who despise the rights of man, and conduct themselves with all the barbarity and rapacity of the German foot soldier.

The language of this gentle, scholarly man became heated:

> With my own eyes, I have seen the systematic burning of
> defenseless villages . . . every crime imaginable and worst
> of all, the crime that they're most noted for, the rape and
> degradation of women hostages. A profound hate has
> arisen in me against this perverse race of hypocrites incap-
> able of nobility or generosity. Do not believe at my age I
> have given in to wounded pride or false patriotism—no,
> it is as a man, not as a Frenchman that I feel such scorn
> for these thieves.

Laboulaye described the damage to his home in Glatigny—

> The gardner gave them the wine and the wood they de-
> manded and they were content to steal from the wine cellar
> in addition to a few objects from the house which struck
> their fancy. . . .

However, he was stunned by how the invaders had treated the
home of his nextdoor neighbor, Madame La Marquise de la Tour
Dupin—

> Her house was entirely ransacked . . . the family art works,
> clocks and pianos packaged and sent off to Berlin . . . but
> what is all that compared to St. Cloud burned with gasoline
> *the day after the armistice,* in addition to six hundred homes
> destroyed coldly, calculatedly, to show the French that the
> Prussians take war *seriously* without *romanticizing* it . . . I
> doubt, if far from France you can get a clear idea of our
> situation—as a nation we are very ill . . . I don't know yet
> what role I will be able to play in the National Assembly,
> I am old, tired, without ambition and do not have what is
> necessary to lead a party.

What Laboulaye was overlooking was his own integrity and his
brilliant sense of history, which would ultimately have a profound
effect on the French government.

His letter ended with a denunciation of Bismarck's policies of
"hatred and vengeance" and a prophecy of that inevitable, de-
structive conflict, the World War of 1914:

There is no doubt in my mind that he [Bismarck] is reawakening all the hatreds of cults and race. In a given time a war will erupt throughout Europe to which the War of 1870 was only a prelude.

It was a disturbing letter for John Bigelow to receive, and when he visited Edouard de Laboulaye in Normandy a month later he found him even more depressed as to the future of France.

Laboulaye confided to him that he felt the political future of France, once freed from Bismarck, was at the mercy of a struggle between the fiery politician, Leon Gambetta, and the party of the late emperor. Attempting to overthrow the Royalists, Gambetta, at that moment, was leading an extensive campaign of propaganda throughout the French countryside, proclaiming that the French owed their land not to Bonapartism, but to Republicanism.

But to Laboulaye, Gambetta was no statesman, merely an ambitious demagogue who aspired to become dictator. What most troubled the exiled senator was that Gambetta wanted a Republic with no constitution. The radical Republican leader wanted to head the government with no restrictions on his power.

Bismarck demanded five billion francs in reparations for the war. It was an enormous amount, but Laboulaye urged the French people to pay it off quickly. Returning to Paris in October 1871, he made a public announcement explaining that, until the money was paid, "the Germans will not leave our territory; until they leave our territory we cannot fortify our frontiers, and until our frontiers are fortified we have no country."

Urged on by Laboulaye, the people of France rallied to raise the money. In the summer of 1871, a subscription for two billion francs was floated to pay the first installment. By the end of the year, it was oversubscribed two and one-half times. Because of France's determination to pay, Bismarck withdrew his army in September 1873, two years earlier than he had planned.

Laboulaye's voice was heard again. He intended to fashion a constitution for the new French Republic. It would be based upon the Constitution of the United States.

In the midst of all this activity, Bartholdi met with Laboulaye on December 3, 1871. Over dinner at the French senator's home in Glatigny, Laboulaye urged Auguste to go ahead with his work on the Statue of Liberty, while he attempted to mount a fund-raising campaign. In the meantime, he had secured for Auguste a commission. During the war, there were many people in New York, especially French residents of Greenwich Village, who had provided aid for those suffering in France. The interim provisional government, which ran France during the Prussian occupation, had chosen Auguste to create a statue of Lafayette to be presented as a gift to the people of New York in gratitude.

Laboulaye saw it as a gesture which would publicize Auguste's name throughout America and open the door for the great gift, the Statue which would soon stand in New York harbor.

Auguste returned to his studio at 38 rue Vavin in Paris. There he was joined by Charlotte Bartholdi, who had left her home in Colmar to be with her son. During the next few weeks, Auguste began planning for the work on the Statue of Liberty.

But Laboulaye could not fulfill his promise to raise the necessary funds. He was too busy helping to reconstruct the government and meeting the demands of Bismarck for war reparations. Auguste had to wait another three years.

CHAPTER

6

Money

EARLY IN the year 1874, a committee called the *Union Franco-Amèricaine* opened a one-room office at 175 rue Saint Honoré in Paris. It was a prestigious address located just off the rue Royale near the Madeleine. Official stationery had been ordered, and at the top of each sheet in gold letters were printed the words:

> Subscription for the erection of a commemorative monument for the hundredth anniversary of the independence of the United States.

The stationery also noted that the president of the *Union Franco-Amèricaine* was Edouard de Laboulaye.

Laboulaye's aim had not swerved—to have the Statue of Liberty completed as a present to the United States in two years, by July 4, 1876—but how this was to be achieved was an unsolved problem. Now, through the press, Laboulaye announced that all contributions for the planned monument could be deposited at the Societé Générale, 54 rue Provence, Paris.

During the months that followed, there were few contributions. One Parisian resident offered ten thousand dollars if the *Union Franco-Amèricaine* should agree to forget about the United States and construct the Statue on the banks of the Seine.

Meanwhile, Auguste completed his memorial to the two dead soldiers in the cemetery at Colmar, finished the bronze figure of Lafayette, and continued to work on the Lion of Belfort.

The Lafayette statue was first exhibited in plaster at the Salon in 1873, to be presented to the people of New York in 1876. It pictured Lafayette at the age of nineteen in officer's uniform, holding his sword against his heart. Standing ten feet tall, Lafayette is thin and youthful, and his stance suggests strong devotion to the American cause.

Bartholdi had also completed three plaster *maquettes* of Liberty, each one larger than its predecessor. His final plaster was four feet tall, and closely resembled the three others, except that, for the first time, Liberty held a set of tablets in her left hand.

As Laboulaye continued in his efforts to raise money to begin work on the Statue, he encountered reactions in France and America which ranged from enthusiastic support to insipid criticism. In the spring of 1875, an article appeared in the *New York Tribune* which poked fun at the undertaking. The editorial began amiably:

> The Frenchmen who propose to erect a colossal Statue of Liberty on one of the islands in our harbor, intend to do a graceful and friendly act, and it would be the height of ill-breeding for us to fail to express a proper appreciation of their act and motive.

Suddenly tongue-in-cheek, the editorial suggested where the Statue might be situated:

> Were the Statue to be placed on the Battery instead of Ellis's or Bedloe's Island, it would be quite as useful and much more satisfying to the public. The thousands of people who will be anxious to write their names in pencil on its legs will dislike the trouble of being compelled to hire a smal boat in order to reach it. If it is placed on the Battery, they will find it easy of access . . . Coney Island would afford another eligible site, where the Statue would be useful, both as a lighthouse and as an attraction and convenience to pleasure-seekers. A lunch-counter and bar might be appropriately set up in its abdominal cavity, and telescopes

could be planted at each eye, wherewith visitors could watch
the shipping. With French and American flags flying from
gigantic hairpins inserted in the Statue's back hair, and
German and Irish flags floating from either hand, the colossal figure would welcome the oppressed of all nations
to come and play three-card monte at its feet. The philos-
opher who should gaze at it from the deck of a passing
steamer could exclaim, "O Liberty! What prize-fights are
fought in thy presence; what whisky is drunk in thy
shadow!"

Finally, the editorial compared the French statue to an American vision of Liberty:

Had Congress decided to erect a colossal statue in our ha-
bor, cultivated New Yorkers would turn grey with anxiety.
Visions of a Statue of Liberty on horseback modeled by a
grave-stone cutter of local political influence would float
before them, and they would hasten to dispose of their
property and to fly the country before the permanent
nightmare in bronze should be placed on its pedestal.

In order to introduce the Statue, and to show what it would
look like, Laboulaye, on October 15, 1875, wrote to William
George Curtis of *Harper's Weekly*, supplying him with an artist's
impression of the completed monument:

Sir,—On the solemn occasion of the centennial anniversary
of American Independence, France, desirous to participate
in the joy of her American brothers, and faithful in her old
traditions, wishes to celebrate with them that noble Liberty,
which represents the glory of the United States, and which
by its example enlightens the modern world. The country
of Lafayette aspires to give a striking expression of affection, which breathes in her heart, as alive today as it was
long years ago. You will see, by the notice herein enclosed,
the nature and character of our undertaking. We cordially
request you to assist us in the realization of our grand and
patriotic achievement. Please, Sir, accept our best feellings.
For the French American Union Committee, the Chairman,

EDOUARD LABOULAYE

A full sketch of the Statue of Liberty was printed on the cover of *Harper's Weekly*. It was the first time that Americans were shown what the French had in mind, even though, due to lack of funding, its construction had not even begun.

On the magazine's inside pages, along with Laboulaye's letter, was the first description of the Statue to appear in an American journal:

> The Statue will be of bronze, more than a hundred feet in height, standing upon a pedestal of the same elevation. The model for the figure, designed by the celebrated French sculptor M. Auguste Bartholdi, has been approved and accepted by the committee in Paris, under whose auspices the project is to be carried out. The pedestal will be decorated with allegorical bas-reliefs, representing the progress of the United States during the first hundred years of their independence. France desires to present us with the Statue; we are to rear the pedestal. Thus, the two great republics of the world will join hands in signalizing by this majestic monument the hundredth anniversary of the birthday of American Independence . . . Rising to the height of 200 feet above the waters of the harbor, this majestic Statue will tower by day against the sky, while by night streams of light will radiate from the head . . . it is not unlikely that next year will witness its realization. The committee, of which M. Laboulaye is chairman, have issued a circular calling upon the people of France for subscriptions to enable them to carry out this grand project. They appeal to Americans to unite with them. The appeal should not be made in vain.

In addition to publishing circulars asking the French people for support, Laboulaye gave a banquet at the Grand Hotel du Louvre in Paris on November 6, 1875. He invited two hundred of the richest, most famous people in the city, among whom were the descendants of Lafayette, famed French general, Jean Baptiste de Rochambeau, and Alexis de Tocqueville. The great hall of the hotel had been decorated with flurries of French and American flags, and at the end of the hall was a dramatic, floodlit painting of the proposed Statue of Liberty shining at night in New York harbor.

The guests were served a fourteen-course menu, which included *Homard à la Yankee* (Lobster Yankee Style). Tributes to the friendship between France and America were given by such guest speakers as Colonel John W. Forney, who represented the Philadelphia Centennial Exhibition to be held the following year, and Thaddeus Washburne, the American minister. Finally, Laboulaye delivered the major address of the evening.

After inviting everyone to join in the great undertaking by giving whatever he could afford, he prodded the memories of the Americans, mostly members of the press as well as the French guests:

> When the delegates met at Philadelphia to declare the independence of the Colonies, they felt that they had but one support in Europe, and that was France!

There was immediate applause.

> . . . When Franklin arrived in France, the first thing he did was to present his grandson to Voltaire. . . . Voltaire placed his hands upon the child's head and said—'God and Liberty!' That was the only benediction worthy of the grandson of Franklin. At that moment France, in turn, sent one of her children to America. I say "child" with reason, too, he was nothing more . . . it was the Marquis de Lafayette. . . .

The two hundred guests listened as Laboulaye began tracing the fascinating career of the nineteen-year-old Marquis de Lafayette—

> Nothing could stop him [though] the French court wished to stop him . . . When the young marquis presented himself to the American representatives, they said to him, "How can we give you service in America when we have no money, no arms, no ships?"

Laboulaye pointed out how Lafayette overcame each obstacle—

> He was in the midst of that crowd of persons always seen during revolutions, men very brave but often full of in-

trigue . . . everyone of whom demanded to be made at least a major-general. Lafayette sent this simple note to Congress: "The Marquis de Lafayette asks two things: to serve as a volunteer; to serve at his own expense. . . . " He was introduced to Washington . . . the American General told him that his men were little used to fine maneuvers and did not have the elegance in the use of arms that the troops of the Continent had . . . "I have come," said Lafayette, "not to criticize, but to learn." From that time there sprung up a friendship which nothing could disturb. . . . Washington, touched by so much candor and modesty, took Lafayette upon his staff and loved him like a son.

Laboulaye recalled the tortuous winter at Valley Forge, how Lafayette was almost fatally wounded at Brandywine, how he returned to Paris in the midst of the fighting—

He was received with immense enthusiasm—he says himself that he was greatly astonished by it. "The 1st of June," he says, "all the ladies wanted to kiss me." Hardly had he reached Versailles before they wanted him to head the army—but it was not that, however, that Lafayette had come to seek in France . . . what he wanted was arms and money for his dear allies.

Laboulaye hesitated. And then in a murmur, he again recalled the young man of nineteen—the evening in 1776 when Lafayette was invited to dine with the brother of the king of England—the words of disdain that the king's brother had spoken—his haughty attack on those American colonists who had declared themselves independent. Quietly, Laboulaye savored Lafayette's famous remark:

On hearing this language, my heart was immediately enlisted. . . .

Laboulaye challenged those present to partake of Lafayette's courage by "enlisting your own hearts." Pointing to the far end of the banquet hall, he begged them all to add to Lafayette's gift by giving money to build the great Statue whose glowing portrait "looms so promisingly among the lights of New York harbor."

The banquet was a success. By the end of the evening, the first funds to start work on the Statue had been raised.

On a chilly November morning two weeks after Edouard de Laboulaye's fund-raising speech, Auguste met in the workshop of Gaget, Gauthier et Cie with twenty members of *Les Compagnons,* the most famous guild of craftsmen in France. Founded in the eleventh century, this confraternity of skilled experts traveled all over the world to ply their arts, carving statues out of marble, erecting cathedrals and building monuments of stone. Trained as apprentices for three years before assuming their professional roles as carpenters, copper-workers, and artisans in such fields as stained-glass windows and gold and silver smithery, they had recently completed the statues and spires on the roof of Notre-Dame Cathedral. There was Baron, the burly head of the molders, Simon, a passionate young sculptor, Bergerat, the foreman of the copper beaters.

Auguste spread his drawings on a huge table beside his four-foot clay *maquette* of the Statue. The craftsmen stood around the table, sipping from mugs of steaming coffee and listening closely as Auguste described how the four-foot *maquette* would be duplicated five more times, each model twice the size of the prior one, until the final enlargement stood one hundred and fifty-one feet tall. The final assembly would be taller than Notre-Dame Cathedral, taller than the Arc de Triomphe—taller than any building in Paris.

Because of the Statue's enormous size, Auguste had long before rejected the possibility of either stone or bronze as being too heavy. He visualized the body covered with thin copper sheeting, like skin. The prominent architect, Viollet-le-Duc, suggested that the Statue be filled with sand to give it support.

It was an historic moment as the twenty craftsmen of *Les Compagnons* gathered around Auguste, watching him study the figures from his charts . . . the first enlargement had to be 2.85 meters in height, 1/16th scale, to a final enlargement of 46 meters—with fine wires leading from 300 main points on the second enlargement to 1,200 points on four plaster sections . . . and the copper sheeting, pounded so thin, until it was less than 2.5 millimeters thick.

Charles Gounod resided in an opulently furnished four-story house in the Place Malesherbes. His white beard and the cap he constantly wore gave him a benign, patriarchal appearance. Composer of the popular "Ave Maria," this famed personality was often referred to as "L'Abbé Gounod." In fact, he had briefly studied for the priesthood when he was eighteen.

After he left the seminary, there was a radical change in his nature. He embarked on a series of sensational love affairs with some of the most prominent ladies in opera, including the English singer Georgina Waldon. By the time he was in his forties, he had a reputation as an insatiable womanizer. In addition, he had been acclaimed one of the world's greatest composers, following the premiere of his masterpiece, *Faust,* in 1859. Another success, his opera *Romeo and Juliet,* was presented in 1867.

Gounod was an extremely handsome man with a broad, powerful forehead, clear blue eyes, and an athletic figure. He had always been an outspoken advocate of Liberty, and in 1875 had bitterly remarked in a French newspaper:

> And what has this century done, I will not say for the pleasure, but for the happiness of the human race? Napoleon! Napoleon III! William of Prussia! Waterloo! Repeater rifles! Krupp guns!

On an afternoon in December 1875, Auguste left his drawings in the workshop at 25 rue Chazelles and traveled across Paris to visit Charles Gounod's home. As always, there was money to be raised, and Auguste met for several hours with the famous composer. During the visit, Auguste persuaded Gounod to create a cantata honoring Liberty for a benefit at the Paris Grand Opera celebrating the hundreth anniversary of the friendship between France and the United States.

The fund-raising campaign was gaining momentum. Auguste had made a trip through the country asking for donations. One hundred and fifty municipalities contributed. The chairman of the Philadelphia Centennial Exhibition, Colonel John W. Forney, invited Auguste to attend the Philadelphia Exhibition as an official French delegate. Auguste now planned to complete the right hand holding the torch, and to have it displayed in Philadelphia on the anniversary of America's Independence. He told his men to stop work on the Statue's body and concentrate on the torch and the right hand.

The benefit performance celebrating one hundred years of friendship between France and the United States, featuring Charles Gounod's "Liberty Cantata," took place at the Paris Grand Opera on April 25, 1876. Beyond the mirrored foyer with its paintings by Boulanger, above the great staircase glistening with hues of white, blue, green, red, and rose marble from all the quarries of France, Laboulaye stood on the one hundred and sixty-two-foot-wide stage. Before a celebrated and wealthy audience of two thousand, seated in the red plush opera house bordered by eight gigantic columns painted with gold, he gave an impassioned fund-raising speech. He drew a sharp distinction between Auguste's version of Liberty and the voluptuous, half-nude female leading a revolutionary force over a battlefield of dying men in Eugene Delacroix's painting, *Liberty Leading the People,* displayed in the Louvre:

> This Liberty will not be the one wearing a red bonnet on her head, a pike in her hand, who walks on corpses. It will be the Liberty who does not hold an incendiary torch, but a beacon which enlightens!

Once again, Laboulaye was prophetic:

> One century from now America, with an enormous population, will celebrate its second centennial. She will have forgotten us, but she will not have forgotten either Washington or Lafayette. This Statue of Liberty, created in a common effort, will preserve these precious memories which are the links between nations; it will preserve among future generations, like a sacred tradition, the eternal friendship of the United States and France.

As Laboulaye left the stage, Charles Gounod emerged from the wings to conduct his cantata. The largest chorus ever assembled at the Paris Grand Opera suddenly stood up beneath the two-hundred-foot-high crimson velvet stage draperies. Six hundred voices rose toward the magnificent crystal chandelier high above:

I have triumphed!
I am one hundred years old!
My name is Liberty!

CHAPTER
7

Return

AUGUSTE LEFT for the United States to attend the Centennial Exhibition in Philadelphia on May 6, 1876.

Reaching Philadelphia on May 18, Auguste entered a city fluttering with hundreds of thousands of flags. At the train station, he saw a parade of Roman Catholic Germans accompanied by a boisterous brass band. Red, white, and blue fireworks illuminated the evening sky. Everyone seemed to be in uniform. As he approached the center of town, he encountered a parade of Shriners marching in bright-colored costumes. "What would July 4th be like," he wondered, as he wrote to his mother, "if already the city is consumed by such a craze for banners and parades?"

Auguste moved into an apartment on Walnut Street as he awaited the arrival of Liberty's torch from Paris. He felt confident that its appearance would stimulate the support of the American people for his Statue.

But by June, the torch had not arrived. Auguste had left instructions that it be shipped to New York as soon as it was completed.

An intense heat wave drained him of all energy even though, as he wrote to his mother, he took several cold showers a day. During the hottest period, he complained, "I live like a Moslem . . . I do everything at a slow pace."

The Statue of Liberty was finally being discussed in newspapers throughout the United States.

The torch, however, did not arrive.

During the last week of June, Auguste traveled to New York City to speak about his Statue at the Offenbach Supper for artists and writers at the Hotel Brunswick on Fifth Avenue, between Twenty-sixth and Twenty-seventh Streets. Afterward, he stayed in Manhattan as a houseguest of Henri de Stuckle, an engineer employed by the New York waterworks. On July 4, 1876, the hundredth anniversary of America's Independence, Auguste took a sentimental boat trip to Bedloe's Island. He noticed that the tug which ferried him across New York harbor was named *Washington*.

Bedloe's Island took its name from a wealthy Dutch merchant who had owned it in the seventeenth century. On the tiny island's twelve acres, the army had built a land battery of masonry in the shape of an eleven-point star. The battery had been named "Fort Wood" in memory of Eleazar Wood, a hero of the War of 1812, but the cannon positioned on its angular bastions never were fired at an enemy. At various times during the 1800s, the island had served as an ammunition depot, a recruiting station, a hospital, and a quarantine station. Finally, it had fallen into such neglect that the guns were taken away, and the army abandoned it.

As he stepped ashore, Auguste remarked to his friend Henri de Stuckle that it would be nice if Bedloe's Island were renamed "Liberty Island."

By the middle of July 1876, Auguste had returned to Philadelphia. On July 14, Bastille Day, he wrote to his mother that the Philadelphia Centennial Exhibition had opened and the French delegation was already on its way back to Paris. He complained that he would have to stay in the United States because "I'll receive my wretched arm only on August 1st."

In the Paris workshop of Gaget, Gauthier et Cie at 25 rue Chazelles, the twenty members of *Les Compagnons* had labored twelve hours a day for months to complete and join together the twenty-one sections of the hand holding the torch.

It did not arrive by August 1.

Weakened by heat, Auguste left Philadelphia. He now had no idea when, or if, the torch would ever arrive. He had to get away, to find a less trying environment where he might escape from his anxieties.

Stopping to visit John and Margaret La Farge in Newport, he continued on to Montreal to be alone. There, he was suddenly stricken with nervous exhaustion.

CHAPTER
8

The Dawn

It overwhelmed me when I saw him again, his eyes rested upon me with so much sweetness that I could not prevent myself from bursting into tears . . . I think that she who shares his life will be very happy, but I see her rich, beautiful, with many talents, in other words, a perfect woman worthy of him. Myself, I have nothing but my heart.

—From a letter written by Jeanne-
Emilie Puysieux to Charlotte
Bartholdi, December 16, 1876

AFTER BECOMING so ill that he had to call for a doctor, Auguste sent a telegram to John La Farge.

A day later, the hotel bellboy came to his room to tell him that a lady sent by Mr. La Farge wanted to see him. It was Mrs. La Farge's cousin.

Auguste woke to see an angel, as he later described the experience, "a kind and smiling face entering my room like a ray of sunshine."

At first Auguste did not recognize her. Five years had passed since he had met her in Newport at the close of his first visit to America. That night she had listened intently as he had enthusiastically described the great project which consumed him. Quietly, she had sat beside him, her eyes shining in the candlelight which illuminated the La Farge dining room.

Her name was Jeanne-Emilie Puysieux.

Now, five years later, as Auguste tossed feverishly in a Montreal hotel room, she tightly held his hand in hers. He barely recalled her luminous brown eyes and long dark hair. She stayed beside his bed all night, and into the next day.

Later, he would remember that she liked to be called just Jeanne . . . that she had been raised in the town of Nancy, which was on the train route from Colmar to Paris . . . that she was the daughter of a wealthy manufacturer, who had lost his fortune . . . that her parents had died, leaving her an orphan at the age of six.

A week later, Auguste was well enough to travel with Jeanne to the La Farge home in Newport. They saw each other every day.

And then, on August 20, the torch arrived.

Auguste hurried to the pier in New York where it had been unloaded. As he accompanied it to the Exhibition grounds in Philadelphia, the *Press*, a Philadelphia newspaper, announced that the whole piece—the torch, the hand, and part of the forearm—was three stories high.

The people of Philadelphia turned out to climb a steel ladder and stand, twelve at a time, on the balcony surrounding the lighted beacon. The *Press* declared that if New York did not provide the money for the erection of the Statue of Liberty, Philadelphia would—that it would rise on George's Hill or Lenon Hill in Fairmount park, awaiting the Centennial of 1976.

With his New York friend Henri de Stuckle, Auguste headed for the Bureau of Copyrights in Washington, D.C., where he registered his creation with the description, "Statue of American Independence." Application number 9939 of the year 1876 was accompanied by two photographs of a drawing of the Statue of Liberty, and a small model.

September was filled with further excitement. On the seventh day of the month, at 4:00 P.M., Auguste's statue of Lafayette was unveiled in Union Square in New York City.

There were parades of soldiers and civic organizations, there were bands and speeches. Mr. Edmund Breuil, consul general of

France, presented the statue in his country's name, and New York Mayor William H. Wickham accepted it for the city.

For Auguste, it was a prelude to what he hoped would occur when the Statue of Liberty was one day dedicated in New York harbor.

The statue of Lafayette was wrapped in an American flag. As Auguste pulled the cord, which released the red, white, and blue veil, hundreds of spectators in the square and the surrounding buildings began to cheer. The two bands present played the *Marseillaise*, and several cannon thundered in salute, while the telegraph wires signaled a regiment of waiting artillerymen in the harbor to join in paying tribute to Lafayette, France, and Liberty. For a full ten minutes, the enthusiasm continued unabated, with the voices of the people every now and then rising above the clamor of music and cannon.

The inscription on one side of the pedestal read:

To the City of New York
France
In Remembrance of Sympathy in Time of Trial
1870–1871

On the opposite side were the words:

As soon as I heard of American Independence
My heart was enlisted

The image of Lafayette as a young French officer holding his sword against his heart inspired a reporter from New York's French newspaper, the *Courrier des Etats-Unis*, to write: "This is really Lafayette, age 19, animated by the ardor of youth and fired by the noble passion for Liberty."

Bartholdi was immediately famous. Invitations came to him from everywhere. On September 19, he gave a stirring speech about the Statue of Liberty as the guest of honor at the Lotus Club of New York.

And then, with his new-found popularity, came a shattering attack.

In its issue of Friday, September 29, 1876, following the arrival

of the torch in Philadelphia, the *New York Times* published an
editorial entitled "The French Statue." Directed against the Statue
and its creator, the tone of the editorial was one not only of
ridicule, but of genuine hostility. It began by stating that, initially,
news of the Statue's arrival had been received gladly, but with
some incredulity. Finally, what had actually arrived from France
was "a section of 'Liberty,' consisting of one arm, with its accompanying hand, of such proportions that the thumbnail afforded
an easy seat for the largest fat woman now in existence."

The *Times* writer had been under the impression that "no less
than 200,000 francs had been subscribed to pay the cost of the
Statue, and that a sculptor had taken the contract to finish it."
But, when only the arm holding the torch was made available,
there was reason to suspect that the sculptor was insane—that he
had started from the top down without knowing what to do next.

The article admitted that "a woman without arms might be of
considerable value. In western towns where husbands yearn after
the privilege of safely wearing long hair, such a woman might be
especially eligible for matrimonial purposes." Perhaps, it suggested, Bartholdi was a charlatan:

> Had the French sculptor honestly intended to complete the
> Statue of 'Liberty,' he would have begun at its foundation,
> modeling first the boot, then the stocking, then the full leg
> in the stocking.

The erroneous conclusion of the article was devastating:

> A dismal report now reaches us from France that work
> upon the Statue has been suspended in consequence of a
> lack of funds. The 200,000 francs have all been expended,
> and it occurs to the Frenchmen that before subsidizing
> another 200,000 francs to complete the work, it would be
> only fair to give the Americans an opportunity to subscribe
> it themselves. From present appearances, we have all of the
> Statue that we shall have unless we are willing to pay the
> cost of finishing it, and it is more than doubtful if the
> American public is ready to undertake any such task.

The editorial estimated that the finished Statue would cost at

least two million dollars. In ignoring the truth, the *Times* failed
to state that America was being asked to supply only the pedestal,
with the people of France providing the required amount for the
Statue itself: "It would unquestionably be impolitic to look a gift
statue in the mouth, but inasmuch as no mouth has been cast of
the bronze Liberty, we may be permitted to suggest that, when
a nation promises to give another nation a colossal bronze woman,
and then, after having given one arm, calmly advises the recipient
of that useless gift to supply the rest of the woman at its own
expense, there is a disproportion between the promise and its
fulfillment, which may be forgiven, but which cannot be wholly
ignored."

What most disturbed Auguste was that he had been pictured
as an opportunist who "had taken the contract to finish" the
Statue. In addition, the false statements that work on the Statue
had ceased and that its completion would require such an enormous amount of money, could prove disastrous to the drive to
raise funds for the pedestal.

Angered, Auguste attempted to answer the attack as best he
could by writing in English to the *New York Times*:

> My dear sir—Will you allow me a few words in reply to the
> article in your paper of Friday, September 29, 1876. . . .
> Your intimation that I have taken a contract to complete
> the Statue is simply cruel. I am in America at my own
> expense, and I have been for the last four months. I was
> in America five years ago for the first time, a quiet observer
> of her greatness and prosperity, and immediately on my
> return to my country, struck by her example, projected the
> work which has now fallen under your severe condemna-
> tion . . . Not one dollar of money will come to me as a result
> of this tribute of the French people to the United States.

He went on to take the editor to task for implying that his
motives were fraudulent and that the Statue was not properly
financed:

> To your attempted ridicule of a stranger and an artist,
> whose admiration of American institutions has always been
> his pride, I beg of you to remember that preparing to place

a Colossus of Liberty on Bedloe's Island, I moved with the cooperation of the French people, with the sanction of the President of the Republic of France and his cabinet, with the aid of all the Republicans in the National Assembly, headed by Edouard Laboulaye . . . and with the aid of 115 cities and districts. The estimated cost of the Statue is 600,000 francs, about 250,000 American dollars. Of this 600,000 francs, more than 1/2 of it has already been guaranteed by the French people.

Citing the names of several famous Frenchmen, including de Tocqueville, as friends of America with whom he now had the honor to be "associated to carry out the great Statue of Liberty," Auguste concluded with a threat:

I have received so many generous words from most of the newspapers of New York, that I am loath to believe that they share your feelings, and I trust that the New York public will soon decide whether this Statue of Liberty shall be placed in their harbor, or whether they will allow it to come to Philadelphia, whose hospitable people welcome me to their hearts and their homes.

The *Times* refused to publish his letter.

On October 5, 1876, Auguste's letter was published in the *Philadelphia Press*, with a note from the editor:

We print below with deep humility that a cause should exist for it, M. Bartholdi's letter to the *New York Times*.

New York Mayor William H. Wickham wrote a letter to the Committee of French Exhibitors to the Centennial Exhibition, which was read at a dinner given for Auguste at Les Trois Frères Provencaux, a French restaurant located in Philadelphia. From Mayor Wickham's letter, it was obvious that not everyone in New York agreed with the *New York Times*. The mayor's letter praised Auguste's statue of Lafayette in Union Square. He then extolled the glories of France's intended gift:

When New York harbor shall be illuminated and adorned

by the colossal figure of which a piece of the arm is before you today, we shall feel that this city is indeed exalted among all the cities of the world.

There were other newspapers which opposed the erection of the Statue of Liberty because of its colossal size, which they found preposterous, and the cost to Americans for its pedestal. But, overall, the nation's press was favorable. The *Boston Globe* happily announced that committees were being formed all over France to pay for the project. The *New York Daily Graphic* admiringly praised Auguste for having "volunteered his services as a sculptor, and entered upon his work without hope of reward beyond that which would accrue to him from the artistic excellence of the work he should accomplish."

Buoyed by such support, Auguste wrote to Charlotte Bartholdi:

> Things are coming along fine . . . When all that is necessary is done, I shall leave with my mind at rest, confident in the future.

"The American Committee on the Statue of Liberty" was formed at the Century Club in New York City. William Evarts, a prominent lawyer, was named chairman, and Richard Butler, a businessman who resided at 10 Mercer Street, agreed to serve as secretary. The other members of the committee included Joseph Choate, Henry Spaulding, Samuel Babcock, John Jay, F.R. Coudert, and the vigorous nineteen-year-old Theodore Roosevelt.

The committee pledged to meet the goal for financing the pedestal, which would amount to $250,000. Auguste wrote to his mother:

> All will go well, and I shall have at least the satisfaction of coming back victorious.

He expected to return to France by the end of November 1876. What he did not tell her was that he had fallen in love.

Since that night in the hotel in Montreal, he and Jeanne had been inseparable. They were living together in New York, while she accompanied him to fund-raising dinners, celebrations, and trips to Philadelphia and Newport.

Sensing that, in addition to his work, there might be something keeping him away from her for so many months, Charlotte questioned Auguste concerning a chance remark he had made about Margaret La Farge's cousin.

Auguste replied:

Is there not a cousin at the La Farge's? Yes, there is one—

Immediately trying to play down the relationship, he asked:

—But, would you like her? I think that you would in some respects, but this is no brilliant match. There is neither wealth, nor beauty, nor social connections, nor musical talents.

Auguste revealed how he had been ill as a result of the hot climate and his fears for the Statue of Liberty—so ill, that in Montreal, he had summoned a physician.

The story of Jeanne followed. She had come to his room. She had nursed him through the night. The warmth of her hand reaching his "gave me an added feeling of comfort. I felt as if she had been sent by you."

Auguste added that, because Jeanne had missed a carefree youth, the simplest pleasures filled her with happiness. When she laughed, she looked only twenty years old.

Charlotte Bartholdi was barely able to endure the shock of her son's letter. He was thousands of miles away, having a love affair with a woman she did not know. She was faced with a problem, which had to be immediately resolved. Rushing to the telegraph office, she cabled a one-line message: "If she is a Catholic, defer the outcome."

Charlotte had raised Auguste as a Protestant, and it was essential to her that he marry a lady of the same faith. She was nervous, never having resolved her bitterness over her son Charles's affair with Fanny Dreyfus. She finally suggested that Auguste return with Jeanne so that they could be married in Colmar.

Auguste lessened his mother's fears by assuring her of Jeanne's religious background: "She is a Protestant, a Unitarian."

Margaret La Farge, at the same time, was urging Auguste to

marry Jeanne in Newport. She insisted that she could not allow the lovers to live under her roof unless they were wed.

Jeanne, herself, was in a frenzy. Afraid that Charlotte would dislike her, that she could not measure up to the sort of wife Madame Bartholdi had envisioned for her son, she impulsively poured out her feelings in a letter to her prospective mother-in-law:

> Very honored and dear Madam: I do not know how to go to the depths of the feelings which confront me; at this moment I feel my heart open to you. I would like to speak to you of happiness, out of the anxiety I am experiencing . . . I am filled with desire to be worthy of your son, and you. I cry over it, I can no longer control it, and I am completely tormented. I never had a real mother to care for me in my childhood, nor did I receive the affection which normally envelops all children. . . . Except with my excellent cousin and friend Madame La Farge, I never found a tender affection. If I could have the happiness to be what you desire for your son, I would be the happiest being on earth.

Jeanne related her meeting with Auguste in Montreal:

> When I learned through Madame La Farge that he was ill, I ran to the Hotel Richelieu, happy in the thought that I would be able to do something for him. I had the joy of seeing vitality and serenity return to his face. He very quickly returned to normal.

Jeanne and Auguste returned to Newport. Her anxiety had begun the moment Margaret La Farge revealed that Auguste was in love with her:

> I felt myself suffocating. Could he be for me, is it an illusion? . . . And then, he told me that he would be happy with me, that I had become a part of his life. Since the moment this happiness assumed a real form before my eyes, I no longer know where I am, I am happy, and at the same time, terribly upset. It seems to me, for my love, I could be everything I want to be. Then, I turn my thoughts

over and over, and no longer find answers . . . my mind
is going to seem deranged to you, but it is my torment
which is the cause. . . . You will help me, won't you? . . .
If I am going to displease you, how unhappy I would
be! . . . Excuse me, dear Madame, in all the confusion of
this letter, I am so anxious that I cannot finish.

A cable arrived from Charlotte Bartholdi. It read simply:

Happy, satisfied, agree, approve of marriage, a second letter will explain.

Auguste had been in New York when the cable arrived, and he
hurried to the La Farge residence to find Jeanne. When she saw
him, she burst into tears. Margaret La Farge began to cry. Auguste
was unable to control himself. Openly, he, too, wept with joy.

But there had been a misunderstanding. Charlotte Bartholdi
had expected Auguste and Jeanne to be married in Colmar. She
was stunned to learn that the marriage would be performed in
Newport on December 20, 1876. When she begged her son to
reconsider, Auguste wrote back: "Impracticable. Shall return
home end of January."

On December 19, 1876, as Charlotte Bartholdi stood at the
counter of the telegraph office to send a cable to the newlyweds,
she felt as if all her dreams had been shattered. Except for the
times she had been with her son Auguste, she had lived a lifetime
of loneliness. Now he, too, had left her.

She wrote the words of congratulations. Suddenly, she began
choking for breath. Grasping for the desk, she lost her balance,
and fell to the floor in a fit.

CHAPTER
9

Marriage

BEFORE UNITARIAN minister Charles T. Brooks, Auguste and Jeanne were married at the La Farge home in Newport on Wednesday afternoon, December 20, 1876. Jeanne was described in the newspapers as "the cousin of distinguished American artist, Mr. John La Farge." The guests were limited to the La Farge family.

There was no word from Charlotte Bartholdi.

Two days later, Auguste was extremely agitated. He still had not heard from his mother. Finally, a letter arrived the following week. In Charlotte's shaky hand, it described how she had gone to the telegraph office on December 19 to cable her congratulations and had suffered a fit. The fit was so severe and unexpected that she was unable to write anything. She had to be taken home.

She explained that she was now fully recovered, and had already ordered wedding announcements, printed in French, to be sent to members of the family and friends. She could not resist adding how much she would have liked to be "with her Auguste at this solemn moment of his life."

Having captured the love of her life, on January 5, 1877, a more confident, almost saucy Jeanne wrote to Charlotte Bartholdi:

My Dear Maman—
Now I am allowed to address you this way. I am your
daughter, and want to be like Auguste, your beloved
child. . . . I am impatient to be near you, to leave this
unease behind. Everyone with whom I have shared my
anxiety reassures me, and tells me that I will please
you . . . but I will only be happy when you have held me
in your arms and told me I am the daughter you
promised to love. Then, only then, will I have nothing
left to desire. . . . I have attended several small soirees
these past few days. Can I tell you, without being
pretentious, all the world wanted to have me? I thought
only of how I owed all this to Auguste. . . . How I regret
from the bottom of my heart that you were not there. It
seemed to me that I was taking your share of happiness.
But, in the end, I promised myself to have you
participate by telling you how I felt about it—between
two good kisses! . . . I would like to understand you
through your eyes. Every day I study your portrait, but
your eyes are lowered, and so I can see nothing. But it
does seem to me that I do perceive you smiling, and that
my trial is over.

The steamship *La France* arrived at Plymouth, England, on February 6, 1877. From their stateroom, Auguste and Jeanne telegraphed Charlotte Bartholdi that they would arrive in Colmar in
less than a week, following a brief stopover in Paris. They were
unaware that Charlotte had already traveled to Paris and was
awaiting them with foie gras and fruit from Alsace.

She had taken Auguste's bachelor apartment at 38 rue Vavin
and decorated it with flowers for her son and his bride.

Before leaving Newport, Auguste had written of Jeanne's desire
to please:

On Christmas Day, when we left church she told me: "I did
not understand the minister, but I prayed all the time for
your mother to like me."

The question was whether Jeanne's need to be accepted would
be viewed by Charlotte as engaging or unattractive. Both women
had experienced extreme loneliness. Jeanne had been orphaned

young, and she was reaching out to a seventy-six-year-old woman who had never had a daughter. And now, Charlotte Bartholdi responded to Jeanne as to a daughter.

In Philadelphia, the Centennial Exhibition had ended, and the Statue's torch, prior to the return to Paris, was dismantled and sent to New York. At New York's largest and busiest intersection, where Fifth Avenue crossed Broadway and Twenty-third Street, the torch was re-erected in Madison Square Park. There, amidst the shouts of drivers, the crack of whips, and the neighing of horses pulling omnibuses, carriages, and wagons filled with beer and produce, thousands of New Yorkers paid fifty cents a ticket to climb the three stories to the balcony surrounding the torch's lighted beacon.

The United States Congress had unanimously accepted the gift of the Statue of Liberty from France. Although it had refused to provide funds for the Statue's pedestal, Congress had agreed to provide a site on which the Statue would stand, once it was completed. The famous Civil War figure, fifty-seven-year-old General William Tecumseh Sherman, had been appointed to decide whether Bedloe's Island, or Governor's Island, would be the site for the Statue.

To Auguste, there had always been only one choice. On Governors Island, the Statue would blur with New York and Brooklyn and compete with the Brooklyn Bridge behind it. But on Bedloe's Island it would stand isolated from every viewpoint. Neither with her back to the New World, nor her face toward the sea, the Statue would stand in profile, watching those passing by her, guiding them as they moved through the harbor.

During his first trip to America, when he met with Senator Sumner and President Grant, Auguste had expressed his desire to have Liberty erected on Bedloe's Island. To everyone who asked, before each group that he addressed, he was adamant about where his Statue should be placed.

During the last week of February 1877, Auguste learned that General Sherman agreed with him.

Funds for the Statue were still pitifully inadequate. In France, a license was secured from the Ministry of the Interior to hold a grand lottery on June 27, 1877. The site chosen was the *Magasins Reunis*, a spacious department store located in the Madeleine in

Paris. There were 528 donated prizes, including a silver plate set worth sixteen thousand dollars.

The lottery proved successful: three hundred thousand tickets were sold at one franc each, which amounted to a total of one hundred thousand dollars.

Auguste was at work on the Statue's head, which he was rushing to complete for the Paris Universal Exhibition in 1878. The span from chin to forehead would be seventeen feet, the nose four and-a-half feet long, and each eye three feet wide. While working on the expression of the face, he was moved by feelings more personal than America's independence, or the loss of his native Alsace. He saw before him the political degradation of his beloved mother. He could not forget her bondage, her refusal to leave her home when it was taken over by the Germans. What he finally sculpted was the face of a courageous woman at whose feet lie the broken chains of tyranny. The face of Liberty became the face of Charlotte Bartholdi.

But it was the body of his colossus which most troubled him. No sculptor had ever created a statue which soared three hundred feet into the air. Even that other colossus, which had stood astride the harbor leading to the ancient Aegean Island of Rhodes, was reported to have risen less than a hundred feet.

Back in 1875, the prominent French engineer Eugene Viollet-le-Duc had proposed that the Statue be filled with sand. He was positive that this would support the Statue's weight.

Bartholdi was an artist whose knowledge of engineering principles was slight, and he began building the Statue before he was certain how it would be supported. Viollet-le-Duc's plan to divide the Statue into a system of interior compartments, or *cloisons*, so that the sand could be removed to give workmen access to parts of the Statue which might become damaged, seemed feasible. But in 1878, Viollet-le-Duc died before he could carry out his plan.

In 1879, a solution came from another source. Fortunately for Auguste, the fate of his Statue's inner structure fell into the hands of one of the most brilliant engineers the world had ever known, Gustave Eiffel.

PART
II

The Genius

CHAPTER

10

Eiffel

IT WAS June 1858.

The young man was solely in charge of constructing a sixteen-hundred-foot cast-iron bridge across the turbulent waters of the Garonne River near Bordeaux. Though he was supervising several hundred workmen, Gustave Eiffel had never constructed a bridge before. He was not even an engineer; three years earlier he had graduated from the Ecole Centrale des Arts et Manufactures in Paris with a degree in chemistry.

The bridge had been financed by the Compagnie d'Orléans and the Compagnie du Midi in order to join their two railroad lines at the Garonne River. The $600,000 contract stipulated that the bridge had to be finished by June 1860. Eiffel soon realized that he was faced with an impossible deadline. The piles supporting the bridge had to be sunk in eighty feet of rushing water.

Working sixteen hours a day was not enough. The twenty-five-year-old former chemistry student was forced to devise a method that had never before been tried. Carefully, he plotted each detail: if he were to use hydraulic presses and compressed air, it might be possible to sink the piles without excavation, saving weeks of labor. Within hours of his discovery, he put his method to the test.

One incident almost disrupted his schedule. On a freezing February morning, a riveter fell into the Garonne and was caught in its current. Eiffel, a strong swimmer who had won a bet when he was twenty by swimming the Seine at night, tore off his shoes and his dresscoat. Plunging into the rushing waters, he located the man beneath the river's surface and dragged him to the bank.

Eiffel climbed out of the water and gave a short speech of warning to the workers on the shore. He then stepped back into his shoes and calmly buttoned his dresscoat over his dripping shirt and trousers.

The two railroad lines were joined over the Garonne ahead of time. The workers chipped in to have a gold medal designed, which they presented to Eiffel with their admiration. It pictured the completed bridge and a hydraulic pile driver.

Twenty-four years later, in 1884, Eiffel completed the engineering of the Statue of Liberty. In 1889 he constructed his most famous, and final, project, the tower on Paris's left bank, which bears his name. At first, both structures were rejected by the public and attacked in the press. But in the end, one became the symbol of America, and the other of Paris.

Before the huge iron girders of the Eiffel Tower began stretching toward the sky, a letter was written to the Minister of Public Works by forty-seven French citizens, including Alexander Dumas, the younger, and Guy de Maupassant. It resembled in intensity the protest of the *New York Times* against the Statue of Liberty:

> Writers, painters, sculptors, architects, passionate lovers of the heretofore intact beauty of Paris, we come to protest with all our strength, with all our indignation, in the name of betrayed French taste, in the name of threatened French art and history, against the erection in the heart of our Capital of the useless and monstrous Eiffel Tower, which the public has scornfully and rightfully dubbed the Tower of Babel . . . When foreigners visit they will cry out in astonishment, "Is it this horror which the French have created to give us evidence of their vaunted taste?" They will be right to mock us, for the Paris of the sublime gothic will have become the Paris of Monsieur Eiffel.

In response, Eiffel commented simply in the newspaper *Le Temps*, "I believe that the tower will have its own beauty."

The public attitude did change and the French began to appreciate Eiffel's magnificent gift. His tower not only made him several million dollars but eventually became the symbol of Paris, herself.

But this was not why Eiffel had constructed it. Bismarck's cruelty to Paris, cutting its people off from the world in the spring of 1871, was an incident which Eiffel vowed would never reoccur. Should France ever again be occupied by a foreign power, from his tower Paris would continue to communicate with the world by radio signals.

In the years that followed, Eiffel failed in his attempt to complete the Panama Canal and was threatened with disgrace. But nothing could stop him. He became a pioneer in aeronautics, designing the jet airplane wing. He envisioned skyscrapers of glass and steel dominating future cities.

But it was his first bridge over the Garonne River in 1860 which gave him a reputation. He had become an engineer—a title that he seldom used. He much preferred to be known as a *specialiste*. . . .

Dijon, France, was located thirty miles west of Colmar. In this city of one hundred thousand inhabitants, Gustave Eiffel was born December 15, 1832, two years before Auguste Bartholdi. Their childhoods could not have been less alike.

There was no question, while he was growing up, that Gustave would take over the family vinegar distillery from his uncle, Jean-Baptiste Mollerat. Mollerat, a passionate Republican, enjoyed the local reputation of having seen Robespierre guillotined. Eyeing young Gustave through a glittering pince-nez, he would rasp, "All kings are rascals," emphasizing the point with a stern glare.

Gustave hated schoolwork, which was taught at the Lycée Royal by rote. But in his first year, two of his professors aroused within him a love of history and literature, which encouraged him to achieve the most difficult of degrees, a double baccalaureate in literature and science.

He was sent by his family to the College Sainte Barbe in Paris to prepare for the Ecole Polytechnique. While in Paris he discovered dancing and met his first English girls. "They're lots of fun," he wrote home. "Much less reserved than French girls."

Every well-to-do bourgeois family desired that their son might enroll at the Ecole Polytechnique. Founded in 1795, its faculties of science and mathematics were considered the most prestigious in the world. But due to Gustave's failure on a final examination at the College Sainte Barbe, the Ecole Polytechnique would not accept him.

His parents were devastated, but Gustave did not seem disturbed. He appeared to have no ambitions other than to prepare for a position in his uncle's vinegar firm. Enrolling in the state-run Ecole des Arts et Manufactures, he graduated without honors in 1865.

However, a disturbing situation had occurred. The Eiffel and Mollerat families had ceased speaking to each other because of a violent political quarrel that erupted between Gustave's father and his uncle. Gustave was no longer welcome in his uncle's business. He was now faced with finding a job in Paris.

Supported by several letters of recommendation, he applied to a number of firms before being hired by Charles Nepeau, head of a company which manufactured steam engines and railway track. Gustave was offered an opportunity to learn the business as Nepeau's personal secretary at a salary of thirty dollars a month.

It was the age of the railroad, and there was a demand throughout Europe for bridges. In the 1850s, eight thousand miles of track were laid and six French railroad companies were formed.

Unfortunately, Eiffel's employer, Charles Nepeau, was unable to endure the competitive pressures. His company went bankrupt, and Nepeau suffered a nervous breakdown. The company was merged with a Belgian railway equipment manufacturing firm to form the General Railway Equipment Company. Gustave was appointed chief of research.

It proved to be a stroke of enormous good fortune. Eiffel's first assignment in this demanding new industry was to oversee construction of the bridge at Garonne.

Meanwhile, Gustave longed for a woman to share his life. After a few unhappy love affairs, he admitted in a letter to his mother, "What I need is a good housekeeper who won't get on my nerves too much, who will be faithful as possible, and who will give me fine children."

Gustave, too, had a forceful mother, and, as in the case of Auguste Bartholdi, he wrote to her constantly. Catherine Eiffel soon found her son the ideal bride, the daughter of one of her husband's business associates, a Mademoiselle Marie Gaudelet.

Marie was seventeen. In addition to being petite, affectionate and dark-haired, she came with a large dowry. She and Gustave were married in 1862 and settled in a comfortable flat in Paris. They had five children before Marie died at age thirty-two.

Gustave never remarried. Marie had fulfilled his needs, leaving him with a large family. Whatever other women appeared in his life were kept in the background.

Gustave's prime concern had always been his work. In 1867 he had opened his own metal-working shops, G. Eiffel and Company, in the suburb of Levallois-Perret, northwest of Paris.

Awarded the contract to construct the iron arches for the Palais des Machines at the World's Fair that same year, he attempted to solve a monumental problem. Up to that time, no scientist had been able to determine the exact principles of elasticity for iron used in construction. Eiffel worked incessantly until he discovered how to calculate the effects of stress and strain on iron structure. His formula, which altered the course of iron construction, enabled him to use much lighter structures without sacrificing strength and rigidity.

Eiffel's company was deluged with contracts to build railroad bridges all over the world. Higher bridges were a necessity. With them came the constant risk of death and destruction. In the United States, between 1860 and 1870, two hundred and fifty-one railroad bridges collapsed.

Because he had miscalculated the windload factor, engineer Thomas Bouch was responsible for the failure of Scotland's Tay Bridge in 1879. On a December evening, shortly after the iron bridge was completed, a gale was blowing. An eight-car train began to cross. Thirteen of the bridge's eighty-five spans suddenly folded. The train plunged into the firth below, killing all seventy-five passengers.

None of Gustave Eiffel's bridges collapsed, and not one of his workmen was ever killed or maimed. In addition, no one died of caisson disease while burying foundations in chambers of compressed air, a condition that occurred during the construction of the Brooklyn Bridge. Eiffel's work principles were so perfectly planned and executed that such disasters were impossible. From the day when Eiffel had plunged into the waters of the Garonne to save the life of a riveter, he commanded loyalty. In return, he paid his workers higher wages than they could earn elsewhere.

In 1875, the Portuguese national railway asked him to construct a bridge across the Douro River near the Portuguese town of Opurto. Because of the Douro River's great depth, there was no possible way to erect a pier in the center. A suspension bridge spanning the river's 525-foot width was the obvious solution, but government policy prohibited suspension bridges. Eiffel decided to build from above.

What he designed was the largest arch ever constructed.

Since there was no way that scaffolding could be erected in the middle of the river, Gustave came up with a daring idea. He built the two halves of the arch out toward each other, holding them from above with steel cables attached to piers on the banks. As the two halves of the gigantic arch crawled across toward each other, more cables were added. Two hundred feet above the center of the Douro River the two halves finally met like giant claws.

Eiffel's triumphant arch over the Douro River was one of the great engineering feats of its time. By 1879 he was already being talked about as a mechanical genius.

In 1877 he had completed the Viana Bridge in Portugal, with a one-piece bridge deck mounted on nine masonry piers. It was the largest bridge deck ever completed.

He had constructed the Tan An Bridge in Cochin, China, over a swift-running river which made supporting scaffolding impossible. For the first time he used what he called his "bootstrap" method, dividing the bridge deck into two sections and hanging them over the river until they were joined.

He erected the iron trusswork and exterior of Charles Garnier's dome for the Nice Observatory. The dome was seventy-four feet in diameter, the world's largest. Eiffel invented a device which had never before been tried. He planted the two hundred and twenty thousand pound dome on a frictionless floating ring which permitted it to be rotated easily by hand.

It was Eiffel upon whom Jules Verne had based his novel, *Robur le Conquerant*:

"Citizens of the U.S. My name is Robur. . . . You see before you an engineer whose nerves are in no way inferior to his muscles. I have no fear of anything or anybody . . . When I have decided on a thing, all America, all the world may strive in vain to keep me from it."

Throughout his career, Eiffel's genius was employed to work on only one statue. Appropriately, it was to be the tallest statue in the world.

11

The Partnership

Eiffel's goal was elegance.

—CHARLES LE CORBUSIER

He thought *in materials.*

—PAUL VALÉRY, about Eiffel

It was the architecture of the future . . . an architecture of voids rather than solids.

—LEWIS MUMFORD

STANDING BEFORE the newly married Auguste Bartholdi was a forty-eight-year-old bachelor with five growing children. Eiffel was five feet, eight inches tall, a little shorter than Auguste. He was only two years older, and yet he already had a grey beard and grey hair, which he kept close-cropped and impeccably combed. Eiffel's heavy lidded, light blue eyes expressed serenity, behind which glinted pragmatic exactness. His daring bridges had made him wealthy. In addition to the stately house he owned in Paris, overlooking the Seine, his chateau in Dijon, and his mountain villa in Switzerland, he had recently purchased a luxurious country estate, which he had named "La Chaumiere des Roses."

What attracted Eiffel to the Statue of Liberty project was the physical challenge, the need to invent an inner structure which could stand on its own, without cables or piers. For the Statue to exist in New York harbor, it would have to withstand the pull of gravity and high winds. More complex than a railroad bridge, it demanded a framework unlike any Eiffel had ever built.

Eiffel's experiments with wind stress, a frequent source of error, had caused him to build wind tunnels in order to test models so that he could measure exactly how full-sized structures should eventually be built. He was the first scientist to conduct those experiments which, in his words, allowed "the much-needed intuition of the mechanic" to overcome "the judgment of the engineer." He concluded that:

> Laboratory experiments with reduced models furnish data of the greatest value . . . Certain tests will determine the selection of different parts according to the strength of materials, while other tests will demonstrate questions of equilibrium and stability, taking account of the weight calculated or assumed for each part. In short, the tests furnish all the elements of design.

Eiffel never considered the possibility of masonry or *cloisons* filled with sand to support Auguste's statue. Those ideas had died with Viollet-le-Duc. To this demanding specialist, the answer was iron.

Le Magicien du Fer, the magician of iron, as Eiffel was soon to be called, seemed to know, to love and be engrossed by iron. He wrote about it constantly, praising its lightness and resistance:

> Comparing equal surfaces of iron, wood and stone, iron is ten times more resistant than wood, and twenty times more resistant than stone. It is in huge constructions that the resistance of iron makes it superior to other materials.

His plan was for the body of the Statue of Liberty to be supported by a single, wrought-iron pylon, ninety-seven feet high. It would be constructed in triangles—forming nine levels of horizontal struts—with angle beams, which would project and attach to the secondary structure. Eiffel's first drawing of the pylon showed its potential as a strong, rigid unit. From the top two

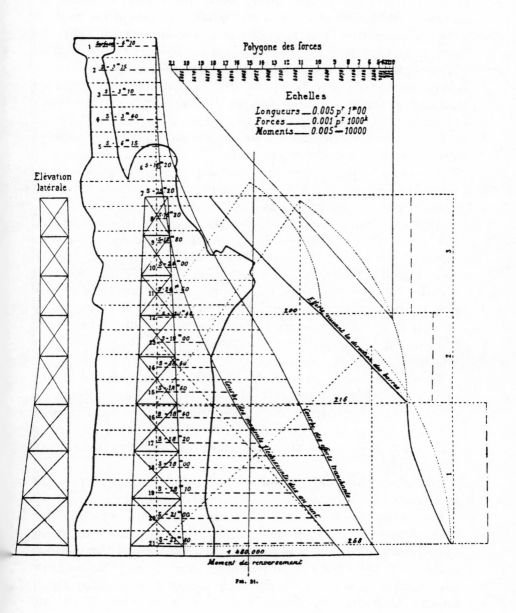

FIG. 21.

levels of the pylon he planned to attach a second pylon, thinner and slightly curved, which would rise another sixty-five feet. The Statue's arm holding the torch was Eiffel's greatest problem. Suddenly it jutted out from the body at a precarious angle. What he attempted to do with this second pylon was to increase the number of triangles to give it strength and then reinforce its rising cross-braces with a massive build-up of iron platework half an inch thick. The result would be an iron structure with extraordinary resilience.

It was certainly the boldest design anyone had invented for a structure weighing 450,000 pounds.

Eiffel's drawings of the arm holding the torch—showing the second pylon—picture it as a giant spring that could actually move, opening and snapping shut as it was buffeted by the wind.

As Auguste had designed it, the Statue would be covered by a thin metal skin of copper (Eiffel called it "an envelope"). The method of attaching the skin to the central pylons would have to be equally ingenious.

Eiffel conceived of angle-irons, reaching out from the central pylons toward the interior surfaces of the Statue's skin. A webbing of iron strapwork, one-half inch to one-and-a-half-inches thick, was riveted to the inside of the skin, and the angle-irons were attached by thin, flat iron bars.

These bars would prove to be the most innovative part of the design. Bending upward and outward, as a result of their connection to the angle-irons, the bars would act like springs, causing the skin to float. Such elasticity would allow the skin to expand and contract in heat and cold, while resisting the pressure of strong winds.

Eiffel had uncannily prophesied stressed-skin construction, the most essential element of airplane wing design.

But, what would most interest nineteenth-century engineers and architects, as they pioneered new forms of buildings made of masonry and iron, was the fact that no part of the Statue's mammoth shell rested on anything below it. It hung solely from the Statue's framework. At the same moment that builders were attempting to discover how to erect skyscrapers in New York and Chicago, Eiffel had found the answer. In the center of the Statue of Liberty, he had brilliantly designed the first great curtain wall

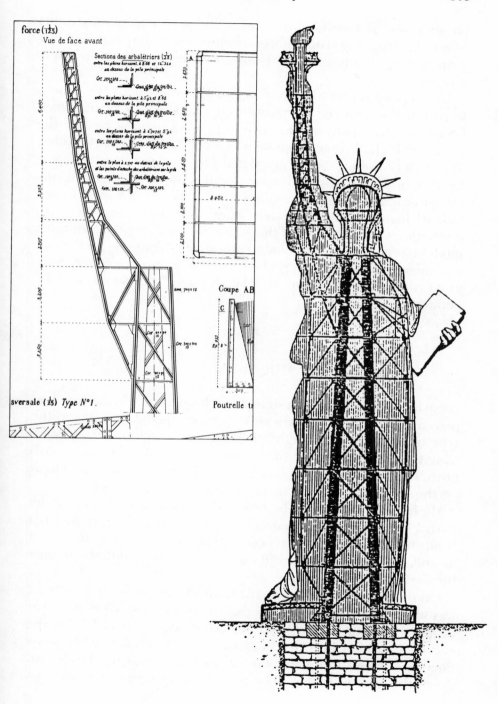

construction. His method of construction, where the components of a structure hung from an iron framework in the center, rather than resting on a foundation below, became the basis of the sky-scraper.

In Auguste Bartholdi's spacious studio at 38 rue Vavin, there were a half-dozen velvet upholstered chairs, and a piano which Charlotte often played, while Auguste accompanied her on the violin, as he had done since he was a child. After Charlotte left to return to Colmar, Auguste invited many of his friends to meet his new bride, including his new-found associate, Gustave Eiffel. He admitted to them that among the things which had attracted him to Jeanne were her lovely arms. Just as he had used his mother's face for the face of the Statue, Jeanne's arms became the model for her arms. The commemorative tablet in her left hand was inscribed in a manner which combined common American usage with classical Latin. It gave the date of America's Independence:

July

IV

MDCCLXXVI

Earlier, when he had designed the head of the Statue, he had placed above it a radiant crown with seven spiked rays. It was the type of crown used in eighteenth-century religious art, symbolizing the sun providing radiance to the seven planets. But in Auguste's interpretation, the seven rays of Liberty's crown shed light on the seven seas and the seven continents of the world.

He had intended that the head and crown be exhibited at the Paris Universal Exhibition on May 1, 1878, to help raise the final funds for the Statue's construction. But, as in the case of the torch in Philadelphia, the head and crown were not completed in time for the opening ceremonies.

On the morning of June 1, 1878, the enormous forty-foot head was loaded onto one of the largest drays in Paris. Twelve horses dragged it from the workshop of Gaget, Gauthier et Cie on the rue de Chazelles into the Boulevard de Courcelles. Thousands lined the streets to watch as it was carried across the Etoile and down the avenue Kleber. The procession of horses and men accompanying the huge face and crown crossed the Pont de Passy onto the Champs de Mars where the Paris Universal Exhibition was in progress.

It was here, in 1790, that Lafayette had sworn his loyalty to the law and the nation before three hundred thousand people, as Louis XVI, watching from a nearby window enthusiastically joined in. On the same spot, eighty-eight years later, Auguste Bartholdi supervised the unloading of the enormous dray.

Word had spread throughout Paris and the fairgrounds were already thronged with spectators. Hundreds of people were waiting to walk inside the structure and to climb the forty-four steps so they could look out through the crown. The arrival of Liberty's head was a sensation.

12

The American Committee

RICHARD BUTLER was the president of the National Hard Rubber Company, a firm that made tires for carriages, located at 33 Mercer Stret, New York City. He was also the secretary of the American Committee for the Statue of Liberty.

The committee had encountered grave obstacles while attempting to raise money for the Statue's foundation and pedestal. Although the *New York Record* and the *Daily Graphic* were favorable, certain New York papers, including the *Times* and the *Tribune*, continued to ridicule the project and most of the wealthy citizens contacted for donations were apathetic.

Outside of New York the committee found no support at all. The prevalent attitude seemed to be that it was New York's Statue so New York should pay for it.

To make matters more difficult, most of the members of the committee were involved in other activities. The committee's president, United States Senator William M. Evarts, was waging an attack on the corrupt regime of New York politician Boss Tweed. Although Richard Butler kept in constant contact with Auguste, it seemed as if the American Committee had no substantial plan concerning how the funds for the foundation and pedestal would be raised.

Bartholdi agreed to one suggestion—that the committee sell small clay models of the Statue, which he would sign. The price for each model was three hundred dollars. Each of the models bore the committee's seal and an official serial number.

Immediately, people began requesting the artist's signature without purchasing a model. When the requests became too numerous to handle, Bartholdi wrote to Butler:

> I am convinced that these people, not withstanding their desire to own an autograph of the author of the Statue, do nothing toward its completion.

From that moment onward, he told Butler to inform them:

> They may go to the office of the committee to add "an amount" for said specimen of my handwriting.

Even though Auguste was continually troubled by the American Committee's inability to raise money, he increased work on the Statue. More craftsmen from *Les Compagnons* were added, until forty men were steadily employed.

On July 7, 1880, the members of the *Union Franco-Americaine* in Paris gathered at the Hotel Continental to celebrate the $250,000 that had been raised to construct the Statue. An illuminated parchment announcing the raising of the money had been sent to the American Committee with a statement that the meaning of Liberty "will live on, consecrated by imperishable bronze."

The statement was in error. Although Auguste had once seriously considered the possibility of using bronze, he had decided on copper sheeting because it was the lightest possible metal covering. It would have the strength and malleability of bronze, without being as heavy, or as costly.

By the spring of 1881, full-scale work had begun on the Statue's body. From the original clay model, each section of the Statue's form was enlarged in plaster five times, until the erected Statue reached its full height of one hundred and fifty-one feet, from the base to the top of the torch.

In order to be exact, each enlargement required nine thousand measurements.

When the final plaster parts were fully completed, their shape was impressed onto thin, malleable lead sheets. In addition, large wooden forms were built to follow the shape of the full-scale plaster parts. On these wooden forms, thin copper sheets, one-tenth of an inch thick, were gently hammered into shape. The copper was then removed from the wooden molds and shaped against the thin sheets of lead to achieve the closest reproduction possible.

The technique, known as repoussé, was invented by the early Greeks, who had observed that metal could be hammered much thinner than it could be cast. Although hammering on the reverse side was extremely tedious, the Greeks had used the process for shaping and ornamenting patterns in relief.

To cover an enormous statue in copper, using repoussé, was an extraordinary feat, but to Auguste and Eiffel, it was the only way to guarantee that the physical features of the Statue would be reproduced precisely.

The craftsmen of *Les Compagnons* were masters of repoussé. Inside the workshop of Gaget, Gauthier et Cie, enormous arms and hands fashioned of wooden slats jutted at monstrous angles amidst gigantic plaster feet and toes. There was the constant din of hammers pounding, as a cloud of fine, white dust from the huge molds constantly hung in the air. The French newspaper *Le Petit Journal* commented:

> Each part of the Statue is prepared with the use of little wooden lathes, which form an enormous cage of lattice work. On this framework is put a heavy layer of plaster. . . . Later, new wooden moulds called *gabarits* are set on this plaster, and it is on these moulds that the men working with copper operate, bending the rigid metal along all the curves, even the most delicate ones.

Le Petit Journal suggested that on Sundays Auguste should give lectures on the process, charging admission.

The craftsmen of *Les Compagnons* were also introduced by the newspaper. There were the moulders, the sculptors, and the copper beaters, as well as Eiffel, the engineer. No mention was made that he was the same Eiffel who had constructed the world famous Douro Bridge in Portugal and who was at that moment preparing to build a gigantic iron tower on the Left Bank.

Adjacent to the workshop housing Auguste and his men, was a courtyard. There, under Eiffel's supervision, one hundred and twenty-five tons of iron were being riveted together to form the Statue's skeleton. Originally, Eiffel had constructed the Statue's framework in miniature, testing its parts for stress and resilience. Later, he stated:

> In the same fashion as metallic piles, which are subjected to calculations for wind stress, I can give the example of the colossal Statue of Liberty, erected by M. Bartholdi. This Statue reaches a height of 46 meters. Its exterior form is created by a thin envelope of copper simply attached to an interior framework of iron. Each piece of this framework was subject to stress calculations in order to determine that the structure would be resistant to hurricanes.

In the courtyard of Gaget, Gauthier et Cie, Eiffel's slowly growing iron framework awaited the carefully hammered copper sheeting, which would be added a piece at a time.

In July 1882, work had been completed to just below the Statue's thigh, a height of thirty-three feet. Auguste invited the press to a luncheon inside Liberty's right knee, an event which was attended by a group of forty editors and correspondents.

Following the luncheon, Auguste spoke to them of his native Alsace, still under German rule. He explained that, to him, the Statue of Liberty was not only the symbol of friendship between France and America, it also embodied his hope that someday Alsace-Lorraine would regain her freedom.

It was a touching experience, and Adrien Herbrard, publisher of *Le Temps,* was so deeply moved that he remarked in his paper that Auguste had spoken "in stirring words, which found an echo in all hearts."

By contrast, the press in New York was not so sympathetic to the ideals of Liberty. After constant ridicule and attacks, attempts to raise money for the pedestal in America had floundered. Haunted by the fear of not having a pedestal for the Statue once it was completed, Auguste mentioned to Richard Butler, the secretary of the American Committee, that he was writing to U. S. Senator Evarts for aid:

> The committee has requested me today to send an official

letter to Mr. Williams Evarts to express to him all its anxiety—we have had a general meeting and the sarcastic articles of the newspapers have worked up the gentlemen's
fears.

Auguste noted that the people of France had grown to love and
appreciate their gift to America:

The work is now being visited by crowds; much is being
said and written about it and, of course, it will attract more
and more attention.

Sadly, Auguste commented, the people of America still seemed
"apathetic."
But he was wrong.
A man would come forth who would become the Statue's greatest champion. In 1883, he would travel to France to meet with
Auguste. After the meeting with this forceful publisher, Auguste
would convey his excitement to Richard Butler—

My letter to you was just finished when I received a visit
from Mr. Pulitzer, who brings a fresh breeze from New
York.

PART
III

The Publisher

Pulitzer

Your paper isn't worth a hang unless people read it. You must make them read it to make them do things.

— JOSEPH PULITZER

Your paper is magnificent and strong. It is ably edited. It is courageous in its views and its editorial page is the finest in the country . . . You are against fakers; so am I.

— THEODORE ROOSEVELT, in a letter to Joseph Pulitzer

ON A FREEZING February night in 1866, a six-foot-three loose-jointed boy of eighteen, with a prominent hook nose and a chin obstinately jutting upward, huddled beside a fat-bellied wood-burning stove near the front desk of French's Hotel at Park Row and Frankfort Street in New York City. His exhausted dark eyes, framed by wire-rimmed spectacles, peered through the large lobby windows at the snow falling on the gas-lighted streets outside. Although the Civil War had ended six months before, he still wore a faded blue private's uniform. It was all he possessed. Joseph Pulitzer was penniless, hungry and alone.

French's was an ancient hotel with yellowed marble floors and foul-smelling brass spittoons lining its wide, drafty hallways. In the early morning hours its fat-bellied stove tempted many a starving unfortunate. Outside, the temperature had reached fourteen degrees.

Pulitzer had positioned himself as close to the stove as he could manage.

During the first eighteen years of his life, his style of living had drastically changed. He had been born in Mako, Hungary, on April 10, 1847, the eldest son of Philip Pulitzer, a wealthy Jewish grain dealer. With his brother Albert, and his sister Irma, Joseph was schooled by private tutors who taught him French and German. He was always a nervous, excitable boy and when his father died and his mother remarried in 1863, he left home with a single ambition: to become a military hero.

In January 1864, applying for a commission in the Austrian army, Pulitzer was rejected because of his weak eyesight, his fragile physique and his age—he was only seventeen.

In February he traveled to Paris to join the French Foreign Legion.

Again he was rejected.

Arriving in England a month later, he tried to enlist with the British forces in India. Once more he was refused.

But even at seventeen, nothing could stop Joseph Pulitzer. He learned that the United States army was desperate for soldiers. Immediately traveling to Hamburg, Germany, he was recruited by agents for the Union Army. By September 1864, he was in Boston.

Serving in the Lincoln Cavalry, Pulitzer was stationed in Washington during the last few months of the war. He won no medals and was finally discharged. In the fall of 1865, he wandered to New York City which was flooded by returning soldiers searching for jobs.

Day after day Pulitzer walked the streets of Manhattan looking for work, but there were no jobs. By Christmas he was struggling to stay alive.

What finally led him on this grim, terrible night to French's Hotel was desperation. He had nowhere else to go. If he could catch a few hours of sleep he might start out again in the morning . . . he would look for something. . . .

What occurred at that moment unleashed within him a torrent of rage that changed his life.

As he dozed by the blazing stove in the lobby of French's Hotel he felt a hand shake him by the shoulder.

It was the hotel porter.

With a sudden fierceness, the porter grabbed Pulitzer by the neck and spun him around. Pulitzer tried to fight back but the porter was too strong. Choking him, the porter dragged him across the hotel lobby. With a powerful shove he hurled the gangling young man through the revolving door into a pile of freezing snow in the middle of Park Row.

Shivering, Pulitzer lifted himself from the snow. It was the most bitter moment of his life. Humiliated, he adjusted his spectacles. At first, he decided that he would never return to New York City.

And then, with a sudden flash of anger, he vowed that he would return—to that very spot—the corner of Park Row and Frankfort Street, which symbolized the lowest ebb he had ever experienced.

But he would come back in triumph.

A fine Italian silk handkerchief his mother had given him was his most prized possession. On that freezing February night in 1866, Joseph Pulitzer sold it for seventy-five cents and hopped a freight train, intending to head as far west as he could go.

By the time he reached East St. Louis, a week later, he was soaked to the skin by rain and sleet. "The lights of St. Louis looked like a promised land to me," he remembered.

But still he had to cross the wide Mississippi by ferry and did not have money for the fare.

Bargaining with the owner of the ferry, he agreed to work for his passage by shoveling coal into the boiler during several round trips.

Finally, earning his way, he arrived in St. Louis.

Pulitzer walked the streets until he found a job at the Jefferson Barracks taking care of sixteen government mules. It proved to be a more difficult task then he could handle. "The man who has not cared for sixteen mules does not know what work and trouble are," he was often to recall.

A week later he was employed as a stevedore on the river docks. During the next two years, a dizzying assortment of occupations followed—construction worker, fireman on a steamer, livery driver, butler and waiter at Tony Faust's restaurant on Fifth

Street. His restlessness and a desire to learn all that he could prevented his staying long at any one task. At the same time, at night, he began studying, or "reading" law on his own, much as Abraham Lincoln had done.

Chess became his principal entertainment and it was over a game of chess one evening in the chess room of the Mercantile Library on Third Street that he met Dr. Emil Preetorius, editor of the city's German-language daily, the *Westliche Post*. Preetorius was amused by the aggressiveness with which Pulitzer played. The young man seemed to possess such reserves of energy that Preetorius hired him at ten dollars a week to run his newspaper.

Immediately Pulitzer wanted to do everything—write the editorials, report the news, set type, and operate the presses. Working sixteen hours a day, from 10:00 A.M. to 2:00 A.M., his long hooked nose, gangling scarecrow body, excitable Hungarian accent, and shabby clothes became a source of humor to the newspapermen of St. Louis. Henry M. Stanley, who was to become the great African explorer and later a knight of the British Empire, was a contemporary of Pulitzer, although he worked for the *St. Louis Globe Democrat*. Condescendingly referring to him as "Joey the Jew," Stanley described Pulitzer as "the most exasperating, inquisitive and annoying reporter" that he had ever known.

Pulitzer attacked corruption in the St. Louis courts. For decades the courts had manipulated city and county funds so that its judges could illegally profit. Pulitzer's attacks on the courts made him numerous enemies, but his most prominent foe was Captain Edward Augustine, court-appointed superintendent of registration for the county, whose duties included keeping government rule in Republican hands by denying the vote to thousands of white Democrats. (During the Reconstruction Period following the Civil War, Confederate sympathizers, known as "white Democrats," were often denied the right to vote.) As a reward, the courts awarded a contract to Augustine to build a new $500,000 insane asylum for St. Louis County.

Calling the contract illegal, Pulitzer constantly assailed Augustine in print. And then, on the evening of January 27, 1870, he attended a meeting of legislators at the lavish old Schmidt's Hotel in St. Louis. Augustine spotted Pulitzer and came after him. Before everyone present he ridiculed his unkempt appearance and his ability as a newspaperman, calling Pulitzer a "damned liar."

Humiliated, Pulitzer left the meeting. But rage overwhelmed him. He returned within twenty minutes.

Augustine, a large, powerfully built man, was waiting for him in the main ballroom. As Pulitzer approached, Augustine started toward him as if to grab him with his bare hands and smash him to the floor. Pulitzer suddenly drew a double-barreled Sharp's pistol from his inner coat pocket and aimed it at Augustine's stomach. Startled bystanders began to yell. The crowd backed up. Augustine leaped at the tall, thin reporter.

The pistol exploded twice as Pulitzer, pinned tightly by Augustine's great arms, rolled over on top of him, crashing with him onto the floor.

One of the bullets struck Augustine below the knee. The second tore into the floor.

The crowd in Schmidt's Hotel had never witnessed such excitement. Men leaped into the middle of the struggle, pulling at Augustine's arms, trying to grab Pulitzer's gun, to call a doctor, as Augustine, bleeding and cursing, was dragged away.

In police court the following morning, Pulitzer was fined $5.00 and costs of $11.50 for breach of peace.

However, he was also charged with the far more serious offense of intent to kill.

A prominent attorney, Charles Philip Johnson, agreed to defend Pulitzer and arranged to postpone his case until feelings had cooled. By the time Pulitzer received the mild fine of $100, the State Legislature, as a result of Pulitzer's investigative disclosures, had not only abolished the courts, replacing them with elected magistrates, but had deprived Captain Edward Augustine of his $500,000 contract to build an insane asylum for St. Louis County.

During the same year, a French sculptor, Auguste Bartholdi, traveled to St. Louis, and although he did not meet Pulitzer, he told Pulitzer's employer, Carl Schurz, all about the Statue of Liberty he was planning to erect in New York harbor.

Neither of the two men could have suspected that one of the most powerful forces behind the Statue would be young Pulitzer.

In November 1871, a fan letter was received by Charles Anderson Dana, editor of the *New York Sun*. Dana was one of the most inventive newspapermen in New York. His skill at political exposure through bitter caricature, parody, and cutting doggerel had made him famous.

A fan letter to Charles Dana came from Joseph Pulitzer:

> I read the *Sun* regularly. In my opinion, it is the most
> piquant, entertaining, and, without exception, the best
> newspaper in the world.

Dana published the letter, which became Pulitzer's first appearance in print in a New York newspaper. The two men began
corresponding.

Pulitzer wanted to expand his interests. He resigned his job on
the *Westliche Post* and sold his share in the paper for $33,000. For
the next three years he had no steady occupation.

For a while, he considered practicing law. He studied Shake-
speare and went continually to the theater to see his friend, actor
John McCullough, who was touring the country in *King Lear* and
Hamlet. He invested in a Mississippi River project, a large triple-
arched bridge, which made him a substantial profit. He attended
the social events of St. Louis and danced at the fashionable Bes-
sehl's Charity Ball, his black curly hair and long nose bobbing
above the other dancers. He attended the Aristotle Society to study
Plato and Aristotle in the original Greek.

It was not as if he were contemplating early retirement. It was
as if he were awaiting a passionate new side of his life to present
itself.

Finally, in December 1876, Charles Dana offered him a job in
Washington as a special correspondent for the *New York Sun*. Vast
amounts of money had flooded the coffers of candidates Rutherford B. Hayes and Samuel J. Tilden in attempts to influence
the United States presidential elections that had been held in
November. Dana wanted Pulitzer to explore the corruption in
both campaigns.

Living in Washington, Pulitzer unleashed an attack against
Rutherford B. Hayes which branded the newly elected president
guilty of fraud. He charged that the country had never before
been so betrayed as by the money interests and such political
brokers as James M. Wells, head of the Louisiana election board,
and Abraham Herriott, chairman of the Democratic National
Committee, who had offered to sell his influence for one million
dollars. Samuel J. Tilden had actually won the election by over

a quarter of a million popular votes. Yet a Special Electoral Commission, which Pulitzer insisted was bribed by political power brokers, had pronounced Hayes the winner by one vote.

Pulitzer's anger and disillusion swept through his Washington columns. Citing the debacle of Grant's previous administration, he predicted that the country was faced with four more years of political degradation.

In the midst of writing his stirring columns for Dana's *Sun*, Pulitzer was introduced by his friend, Missouri Congressman John E. Clarke, to an exceptional dark-eyed beauty of twenty-three. Miss Katherine Davis, daughter of Judge William Worthington Davis of Georgetown, was a cousin of the Confederate leader, Jefferson Davis.

Pulitzer had no illusions regarding his social status among such families as the Davises. Fearing that he would be rejected, he did not tell Katherine that he was Jewish.

Nor did it stop him from trying to sweep her off her feat.

Katherine Davis suddenly found herself being romanced by a thirty-year-old man who had dreams of becoming rich and famous but with no idea of how to achieve them. His warmth and brilliance contrasted with temperamental bursts of fury and indecision.

But there was no question that he loved her. It was the first time he had fallen in love, and in a letter to her Pulitzer admitted his terrible inner distress:

> I have an ideal of home and love and work . . . I am almost tired of this life—aimless, homeless, loveless . . . I am impatient to turn over a new leaf and start a new life . . . I could not help feeling how utterly selfish men are in love compared with women, when I read your letter and feel its warmth. I cannot help saying that I am not worthy of such love, I am too cold and selfish. . . . Still, I am not without honor, and that alone would compel me to strive to become worthy of your faith and love, worthy of a better and finer future . . . There, now you have my first love letter.

He asked her to marry him and she agreed. The marriage took place in the very formal Episcopal Church of the Epiphany in Washington on June 19, 1878.

Supposedly, Katherine's parents and friends were shocked not by his semitic features but rather by Pulitzer's lack of religious affiliation.

The Pulitzers traveled to Europe on their honeymoon and Joseph continued working as a correspondent for Dana's *New York Sun*. He showered gifts on his new wife, adored her; and finally he admitted to her that he was Jewish. Katherine was extremely upset that he had not previously told her, and he explained that his greatest fear was losing her.

Despite any feelings of betrayal Katherine may have experienced, their marriage survived—for thirty-three more years.

In October 1878, Joseph Pulitzer's assignment with the *New York Sun* ended. He decided to return to St. Louis.

St. Louis had four newspapers, one of which had recently declared bankruptcy. The *St. Louis Dispatch* was being offered for public sale on the courthouse steps at noon, December 9, 1878.

No one wanted the paper with its rundown office at 111 North Fifth Street, its ancient flatbed press and a circulation of less than two thousand, except Joseph Pulitzer, who bid $2,500 and became its owner. Pulitzer had returned to St. Louis in November 1878, with a beautiful pregnant wife and just enough money to rent a home at 2920 Washington Avenue in one of the finest residential areas of St. Louis.

Realizing that his new acquisition, the decrepit *St. Louis Dispatch*, needed a more modern printing plant, Pulitzer approached John A. Dillon, the Harvard-educated, thirty-five-year-old owner of a tiny newspaper, the *Evening Post*, which had been in business for nine months.

The *Evening Post* was also approaching bankruptcy. Pulitzer proposed that they join forces.

The first issue of the *St. Louis Post-Dispatch* appeared on December 12, 1878.

All of Pulitzer's observations and preparation as a newspaperman, his toughness, the bitter years he had hungered to thrust himself forward, suddenly united in a brash burst of determination. His specialty had always been to attack, and in the months that followed no organization, regardless of its political backing, was immune from exposure within the pages of the *St. Louis Post-Dispatch*. His crusades against corruption in the St. Louis gas company, the lottery racket, the horse-car monopoly, and the frauds perpetuated by insurance companies began to sell newspapers. When rich landowners pressured their merchant friends to withdraw advertising from the paper, Pulitzer published a list of their names and the addresses of the houses they had leased to prostitutes. As a result Pulitzer made more enemies than ever before. Soon there were so many threats against him personally that he was forced constantly to carry a pistol.

He was an excellent horseman who usually rode a horse to work, wearing a large felt hat and a long coat. With a pistol at his hip, his black beard, and his dark eyes squinting behind wire-rimmed spectacles, he looked like a combination Jewish rabbi and frontier marshal.

Relentlessly Pulitzer's editorials flayed what he considered America's greatest evil—

> Money is the great power of today. Men sell their souls for it. Women sell their bodies for it. Others worship it. . . . It is the growing dark cloud to our free institutions. . . .

He was a born reformer, constantly fighting for the rights of the individual against the cold insensitivity of greedy institutions. No newspaper editor in America seemed so radically on the side of the common man—

> What is the great demoralizer of our public life? Of course, corruption. And what causes corruption? Of course, the greed for money. And who offers the greatest temptation to that greed? Corporations. . . .

Pulitzer worked sixteen hours a day, far into the night, scribbling articles and editing by gaslight to make the *St. Louis Post-Dispatch* startling and irreverent. He gave it a new, fresh feeling, not found before in newspapers, delighting his readers with stories that they could find nowhere else. When one of St. Louis's leading businessmen died in a hotel room with a woman who was not his wife, Pulitzer headlined the article, "A WELL KNOWN CITIZEN

STRICKEN DOWN IN THE ARMS OF HIS MISTRESS." Parallel to the article was a front-page interview with the unhappy woman.

When a young war hero shot himself, the *Post-Dispatch* printed a passionate letter found on the body. It revealed the unrequited love affair which led to his suicide.

By 1882, the *Post-Dispatch*'s circulation had risen to 22,000, a gain in three years of 1,000 percent, with a yearly profit exceeding one hundred thousand dollars.

Pulitzer shared his new-found wealth with his staff. His reporters were not only the best paid in St. Louis, but every employee received a two-week annual vacation with pay—unheard of at that time. If a worker became ill, his salary continued. In addition, everyone—reporters, staff, pressmen, newsboys—enjoyed the annual Christmas dinner with all the trimmings.

But Pulitzer longed to return to New York and own a newspaper there. It was his plan to continue to run the *Post-Dispatch*, but having a successful New York newspaper became an obsession.

In April 1883, Joseph Pulitzer suddenly arrived in New York with his life savings: $200,000. Taking out a bank loan for an additional $140,000, he intended to purchase the *New York World* from financier Jay Gould.

Jay Gould was a slightly built, black-bearded robber baron whose scandalous business enterprises, such as overpricing blankets sold to the U.S. Army, had made him unpopular with the American public. After making millions in railroads, he had taken over the *World*. And he had just seized control of Western Union.

Gould's *World* was a specialized newspaper, edited to appeal to New York's social hierarchy and to its most successful businessmen. Because of its exclusivity, its circulation was less than twenty thousand.

Gould's asking price for the *World* was half a million dollars, but after several bargaining sessions, Pulitzer managed to acquire the paper for the exact amount he possessed. By May 1, 1883, the *New York World* was his, and with it the fulfillment of the vow that he had made to himself on that freezing February night seventeen years before as he had huddled penniless and starving in the snow. Borrowing on his new investment, Pulitzer purchased French's Hotel on the corner of Park Row and Frankfort Street.

His moment of triumph had come. Razing the ancient hotel, he announced that in its place the offices of the *New York World* would be established—in the tallest, most modern building in Manhattan.

It would take him seven more years, but by 1890, the newsroom and editorial offices of the *World* occupied a great gilded dome. Within the dome Pulitzer's semicircular office with its frescoed ceilings and embossed leather walls had three towering windows giving him a sweep of vision from Governors Island and Brooklyn to the upper East River and Long Island. The handsome twenty-story Pulitzer building not only dominated Park Row, as Pulitzer had planned, but also was the first Manhattan building visible to ships coming in from Europe.

Pulitzer moved to New York City in April 1883, with his beautiful twenty-eight-year-old wife Kate, and their three infants: Ralph, three and a half; Lucille Irma, two and a half; and Katherine Ethel, eight months. To make his glory complete, the young man who had once been thrown out of the lobby of a downtown Manhattan hotel during a freezing storm now took a suite of rooms at the luxurious Fifth Avenue Hotel.

But New York was not St. Louis.

Lining Park Row in Lower Manhattan, New York's dailies occupied an eight-block area similar to Fleet Street in London. Reporters and pressmen caroused in taverns such as White's on Fulton Street and consumed hot chowder and beer in the Fulton Fish Market at dawn.

The competition was awesome.

The citizens of New York had sixteen newspapers from which to choose. They could read the *New York Sun*, the *Herald*, the *American*, the *Tribune*, the *Record*, the *Times*, the *Telegraph*, the *Star*, the *Press*, the *Journal*, the *Daily News*, the *Evening Post*, the *Daily Mirror*, as well as the *Commercial Advertiser* and the *Hebrew Standard*.

In contrast to the *World*'s paltry daily circulation of 15,000 Charles Dana's *Sun* led the pack with 140,000, followed closely by James Gordon Bennett's *Herald*, Whitelaw Reid's *Tribune*, and George James's *New York Times*.

The opening salvo aimed at Pulitzer came from the editor he most admired, his former employer, Charles Dana, who announced in the *Sun*'s editorial pages that he was not reluctant to welcome a "clever man . . . especially when he has once been a correspondent for the *Sun*, which shines for all."

But neither did Dana propose to praise Pulitzer:

> Mr. Pulitzer possesses a quick and fluent mind with a good store of originality and brightness; but he has always seemed to us rather deficient in judgment and staying power.

Pulitzer's response was to sell copies of the *World* for the cheapest price of any New York newspaper.

Although he was always generous to those who worked for him, Pulitzer stringently economized in other ways. He used cheap newsprint and ink and managed to function using worn type. Consequently, he was able to advertise on the *World*'s front page that it was the only eight-page paper in the country priced at two cents a copy.

The *World*'s circulation gained slightly.

The *Times* and the *Tribune*, desiring to finish Pulitzer off and send him flying back to St. Louis, lowered their prices to two cents.

The cocky Pulitzer was overjoyed.

When the *Herald* also dropped its price from four cents to two cents, the *World* announced:

Another victim, another victory for the World!

Dana came back at him in what proved to be the beginning of a battle of invective between the two men. The final explosion was to occur three years later during an election campaign. The *Sun* let loose a torrent of viciousness:

> We wish, Pulitzer, that you had never come. . . . Perhaps your lot will be like that of the mythical unfortunate of the same race you belong to . . . that weird creation of medieval legend, a creation, by the way, far more pre-possessing than you are—we mean, The Wandering Jew! In that case it may shortly please the inscrutable Providence, which has chastened us with your presence, to give you that stern and dreadful signal—Move on, Pulitzer, move on!

Pulitzer responded:

The editor of the *World* accepts the hatred of Mr. Dana as a compliment . . . Sad, no doubt, Mr. Dana is, that somebody came who could provide the New York public with the paper it wanted. But the man is here, and he will remain.

What New York did not have was a strong Democratic newspaper, even though the city was predominantly Democratic. The *Tribune* and the *Times* were Republican, and the *Sun* and the *Herald* were independent. What Pulitzer saw was that none of the leading newspapers appealed to the popular mind.

Pulitzer needed a stirring campaign which would thrust his newspaper to the forefront. Two weeks after taking over the *World*, he was certain he had found it.

The concept of Liberty had always intrigued him, especially the fact that it was so often misused. And yet, to Pulitzer, it was the most vital state of being. As he once wrote in an article for the *Sun*:

> People without Liberty have despots. People with too much have demagogues . . . Both abuse Liberty.

To Pulitzer, society consisted of Liberty and property:

> Socialism means the destruction of the latter [property]. Imperialism to save it would trample over the dead body of Liberty.

He was aware of the struggle which the Statue of Liberty had faced since Auguste Bartholdi had first visited St. Louis in September of 1871. At that time Bartholdi had met with Carl Shurz, one of the publishers of the *Westliche Post*, who employed Pulitzer as a reporter.

The struggle to bring Bartholdi's masterpiece to America inspired Pulitzer. On May 14, 1883, he wrote a strong message to the public:

> The Bartholdi Statue will soon be on its way to New York. The great goddess comes with her torch held aloft to enlighten the world.

His editorial blamed those millionaires who spent money unnecessarily:

> ... here in the commercial metropolis of the Western
> world, where hundreds of our citizens reckon their wealth
> by millions, where our merchants and bankers are spoken
> of as "princes," we stand haggling and begging and scheming in order to raise enough money to procure a pedestal
> on which to place the Statue when it arrives in our harbor.
> New York ought to blush at the humiliating spectacle. A
> quarter of a million dollars only needed for the base and
> the pedestal and the subscription crawling along at a snail's
> pace with the aid of fairs and theatrical performances given
> as for a local charity! The dash of one millionaire merchant's pen ought to settle the matter and spare the city
> further humiliation.

Pulitzer could not resist comparing New York to the city from which he had just arrived:

> Recently, St. Louis wanted half a million dollars for a new
> music hall. The money was raised in a very short space of
> time. If Bartholdi's Statue were to be raised on the bluff
> of the Mississippi, the pride of St. Louis could supply the
> price of the pedestal in one hour.

Pulitzer called for a popular subscription. It was his feeling that the Statue was a symbol of national pride—that it was the duty of every American to support it.

By May 18, only $135.75 had been raised by the *World*.

Pulitzer was in a fury. Angrily he scolded the millionaires:

> How singular that some one or more merchants or speculators who have made enormous fortunes in New York
> do not feel enough pride or interest in the reputation of
> the city to give the remainder of the sum needed for the
> work.

When he criticized the American Committee on the Statue of Liberty in New York for its "remissness or lack of judgment" for not having "obtained from any banker 100 names of men who would on paper have been glad to subscribe $1,000 each and enroll themselves on a list of honor," he was answered by committee treasurer Henry F. Spaulding. After accusing Pulitzer of "laboring under a misapprehension," Spaulding agreed that "some one or more individuals might be willing to contribute the whole cost of it," but he added airily:

> The committee, having the matter in charge, are opposed to permitting this to be done, preferring to make it a national and not a purely sectional affair. It is expected that $150,000 will be readily raised in New York and vicinity out of the needed sum of $250,000. To other cities and towns of the United States is given the privilege to contribute the remainder as a manifestation of their friendship and good will toward the Republic of France. . . . We do not doubt their response when they understand what it means.

What rankled Pulitzer was that in the seven years since the American Committee had been formed, it had not even obtained one hundred thousand dollars.

Again and again his editorials attempted to arouse his readers, until he remarked in frustration:

> More appropriate would be the gift of a Statue of Parsimony than a Statue of Liberty, if this is the appreciation we show of a friendly nation's sentiment and generosity.

The response to the *World*'s appeal was humiliating. There were even fewer donations. Every campaign he had ever initiated since he took over the *St. Louis Post-Dispatch* in 1878 had proved successful. Suddenly, he was spearheading a drive which appeared doomed by apathy.

Amazed, he could not understand how a city with the largest population in the United States, a city that was able to support sixteen daily newspapers, could not come forth with the funds needed.

On June 10 he announced that the *World* would no longer ask for funds, but he promised it would keep the public informed concerning the Statue and its pedestal. Having to end the sub-

scription drive one month after his first appeal was one of Pulitzer's most dismal defeats. He commented bitterly on the *World*'s
editorial page:

> The Statue should be placed on Montmartre where people
> are appreciative of Liberty.

Like the young man of eighteen in the lobby of French's Hotel,
New York had once again challenged him.

CHAPTER

14

The Final Vision

IN THE courtyard of 25 rue Chazelles, Edouard Leboulaye had watched his dramatic wish come to life. Although unfinished, the huge brown figure of Liberty now towered high above the multicolored roofs of Paris. The Statue had become almost a real person to those creating her. The craftsmen of *Les Compagnons* began to refer to her affectionately, perhaps influenced by Auguste, who always called her "my daughter Liberty." She could be seen from the Bois de Boulogne, from the Jardin des Tuileries, from Notre Dame . . . the people of Paris had watched carefully over her birth and infancy as her arms and body struggled piece by piece up Eiffel's two hundred thousand pound pylon, and finally into the skies.

In another year, on July 4, 1884, Laboulaye planned to present the Statue officially to the government of the United States.

The French government had changed. In 1879, the Republicans had taken over the Senate and the National Assembly, and in recognition of his services, especially for his constitution which the nation had finally adopted, Laboulaye had been given a rare honor. He was named senator for life.

Laboulaye also made certain that the Bonapartes were outlawed.

A specific law was passed stating that they would never again be able to return to France as rulers.

Prior to his political involvement, when Laboulaye was a professor at the College of France preaching a love of Liberty and American institutions, in his spare time he had written a series of popular short stories entitled *Contes bleus.*

In 1880, he received a letter from a Brooklyn, New York, school-teacher, Mary Lucy Booth. Miss Booth, who would later write *A History of the City of New York* and would become editor-in-chief of the *New York Bazaar,* had searched for Laboulaye's latest volume of stories but could not find it.

Laboulaye responded:

> I would really like to be able to send you a new volume of my stories but for ten years my life has been so heavy with the misfortunes of my country that I have written nothing. Perhaps in a year or two, if I am in this world, I will be able to send you the last edition of my stories.

During the three years that followed, Laboulaye and Mary Booth frequently corresponded. By 1883 he was seventy-two. The nightmare of the Franco-Prussian war and the decade of feverish activity which followed had broken his health. Despite his country's acceptance of Republicanism, he had become disillusioned with the course it was taking, but he felt powerless to fight any longer. He confided to Mary Booth:

> My health is greatly altered. The life I lead does not sweeten my old age. My countrymen forget the principles of Liberty in order to take up again the authoritarian traditions of despotism. The French Republic moves farther and farther from American ideas. As for me, I remain faithful to them. And I fear, I really fear that we are heading toward the abyss by distancing ourselves from the wise lessons of Washington, Madison and Hamilton. But I finish. They say old men by habit see everything in dark tones.

But there was one accomplishment he could be proud of. Laboulaye was as troubled as Bartholdi at the American Committee's inability to raise the funds for a pedestal—but nothing could stop the dream from someday happening. As he related to Mary Booth, he could see the wonderful gift already looking down on New York harbor:

Viewed from New York and New Jersey, from Brooklyn or from the mouth of the narrows, she appears in true grandeur and will certainly be admired for centuries by civilized people. The Colossus of Rhodes lasted 900 years. We hope that this Statue, erected to commemorate the friendship of France and America, will last until the year 2900.

Although Edouard Laboulaye never visited the United States, he loved everything that was American. His home in Glatigny was filled with patriotic memorabilia. There, on May 25, 1884, eleven days after Joseph Pulitzer's unsuccessful appeal for money in the *New York World*, Laboulaye died, surrounded by presents from friends he had never met, who lived in a country he had known only in his heart.

Auguste was so shaken by the news of his great patron's death, that he was unable to work on the Statue for a week. Laboulaye had given him the dream—then pointed the way to its completion.

Now Auguste would be alone for the final struggle.

Bartholdi's words to Richard Butler of the American Committee for the Statue were simple:

I was greatly affected by this misfortune as I would have been so grateful to have seen him participate in the satisfaction from seeing the work to which he had shown such devotion fully accomplished . . .

A speaker at Edouard Laboulaye's funeral had been the French historian Henri Martin. Bartholdi ended his letter to Butler with one of the statements Martin had made:

Yet we will know how to honor his memory by *our very acts.*

CHAPTER

15

Emma

The Jew is a born rebel. He is endowed with a shrewd, logical mind that he may examine and protest; with a stout and fervent heart, in order that the instinct of Liberty may grow into a consuming passion.

—EMMA LAZARUS

I know little about her work, but her face is an argument—a beautiful face.

—WALT WHITMAN, about Emma Lazarus

As THE Statue of Liberty, which Edouard Laboulaye had named *Liberty Enlightening the World*, was nearing completion in Paris, a pamphlet was published by the American Committee on the Statue of Liberty, located at 25 Liberty Street, room 32, in Manhattan. The pamphlet stated that the chairman of the American Committee was Senator William A. Evarts, that Richard Butler was secretary, and Henry F. Spaulding treasurer. Listing the funds which had been raised for the Statue's foundation and pedestal, an entry in the pamphlet noted that the largest amount, $13,674, had come from "Proceeds of Art Loan Exhibition, New York City."

135

The Art Loan Exhibition had been a benefit organized by a group of artists to raise funds for the Statue's pedestal. It had opened on December 9, 1883, at the National Academy of Design, Twenty-third Street and Fourth Avenue in Manhattan. Original manuscripts by such famous writers as Mark Twain, Brett Harte, and Walt Whitman were auctioned off. In addition, the founders of the event had approached Emma Lazarus, a thirty-four-year-old poet from New York, to write a sonnet.

She refused, at first. Then changed her mind.

Even though very little has been written about Emma Lazarus, what she wrote became one of the most famous and inspiring poems in the world.

Emma Lazarus's ancestors were among the first twenty-six Jews to settle in New York City in 1649, when it was still the Dutch Colony of New Amsterdam, governed by Peter Stuyvesant. The Lazarus family had come from Portugal, by way of Brazil. Emma's grandfather, Eleazar Samuel Lazarus, edited the standard liturgy for the Sephardic Shearith Israel Congregation, the first synagogue in New York. Her uncle, Reverend J.J. Lyons, became *hazzan*, or cantor-minister of the congregation.

The Lazarus family had prospered in New York over several generations. Emma's father, Moses Lazarus, had made a fortune in the sugar refining industry before he retired in 1865 at the age of fifty-two.

In the late 1860s, of New York's population, which totaled 330,000, there were ten thousand Jews. Emma admitted that she was brought up "in a society where all differences of race and faith were fused in a refined cosmopolitanism." The family did observe some form of the Sabbath and holy days, and they attended services on Rosh Hashanah and Yom Kippur.

Moses Lazarus provided his family with an elegant five-story townhouse, handsomely furnished with down cushion sofas and a Chickering piano in the front parlor. The house was located at 36 West Fourteenth Street in the section just off Fifth Avenue known as "millionaire's row." Here Moses and his wife, Esther Nathan, raised five daughters. Emma, their third daughter, was born on July 22, 1849.

Though Moses was a warm, loving father, Emma, from childhood, was cold and self-critical. Her elder sister Josephine described her as "a hidden, withdrawn personality," adding that "one hesitates to lift the veil on so shrouded a life and spirit."

Emma had little interest in being Jewish. When asked by her teacher, Rabbi Guttheil, to write a poem for a Jewish hymn book, she refused, telling him flatly, "I shall always be loyal to my race but I feel no religious fervor in my soul."

As a child, much of her time was spent reading classic literature. She was educated by private tutors who helped her master French, German, and Hebrew. She also developed a clear, vivid writing style.

When she was seventeen her first book, *Poems and Translations*, was published. It contained some of her own poems as well as translations of various works by Hugo, Dumas, Schiller, and Heine.

Ralph Waldo Emerson, the famed essayist and poet, who was in his mid-sixties, was immediately impressed by her fresh, youthful talent, which he found "extremely earnest." Emerson, in addition to such writers as Henry David Thoreau, Margaret Fuller, Amos Bronson Alcott, and Elizabeth Peabody, had embarked on a religious quest, rebelling against nineteenth-century materialism. As the founder of the New England Transcendentalists he idealized the creative spirit as the source of power in the universe. Emerson's efforts contributed to the abolitionist movement, to feminism, to educational innovation. In his essay, "The American Scholar," he defined the new "intellectual" set free from institutional bondage, who could think for society at large. His writings prepared the ground for Whitman, Melville, and Hawthorne, who represented the first flowering of American genius and a permanent source for American literature.

Emerson encouraged Emma to study Thoreau and Whitman.

Emma was nineteen in June 1868, when she responded to him in a letter:

> I have only been reading Thoreau's Concord River and letters, and a poem or two of Walt Whitman—these writers are so in harmony with nature . . . I no longer wonder at your admiration of Thoreau—what a noble, true, bold spirit his must have been—or rather is—for he is now more alive to me than many who are living near me.

When she completed her five-act verse tragedy, *The Spagnoletto*, it was sent to Turgenev, then living in France. He wrote back: "An author who writes as you do is not a 'pupil in art' anymore; he is not far from being himself a master."

But it was Emerson to whom she constantly turned for approval and praise. She held him in awe. She wrote to him in November 1868:

> I wish I could express to you my thankfulness and pleasure on receiving your letter and knowing with what patience, indulgence and kindness you read my unworthy verses. I was as much astonished as delighted at the estimate you were good enough to set upon them . . . I feel so undeserving when I read your letter, that your praise, far from satisfying me with what I have accomplished, will be but an incentive and spur to me, to strive towards something higher and nobler . . .

Six years later her feelings toward Emerson radically changed. He had published an anthology entitled *Parnassus*, which included verse by 165 poets. When he rejected the poems Emma submitted, she reacted in anger:

> I cannot resist the impulse of expressing to you my extreme disappointment at finding you have so far modified the enthusiastic estimate you held of my literary labors as to refuse me a place in the large and miscellaneous collection of poems you have just published. I can only consider this omission as a public retraction of all the flattering opinions and letters you have sent me and I cannot in any degree reconcile it with your numerous expressions of extravagant admiration.

Emma waited for weeks for his reply, but he never answered her letter. Finally, Emerson did contact her—inviting her to spend a week at his home with himself and his thirty-four-year-old daughter Ellen.

Emma accepted the invitation and peace was restored. After all, Emerson had done more than anyone to further her career.

Emma had always felt most at home with Emerson and the writers she met through him. Despite her sister Josephine's dour picture of her as "a hidden, withdrawn personality," Walt Whitman found that Emma had "a great, sweet, unusual nature."

Thin-faced, with a sharply pointed nose and penetrating brown eyes, Emma dressed her small-boned, petite body in conservative, elegantly tailored gowns. She was never active socially, and although she had several male friends, she was shy and introspective.

Few knew the private life of Emma Lazarus.

No one has comprehensively written of the tragedy, the disgrace which affected this brilliant woman who wanted so much to be loved.

The story that has not been told is that Emma fell in love when she was twenty-one with Washington Nathan, a distant cousin on her mother's side of the family. He was twenty-six, had a seat on the New York Stock Exchange, and was highly respected. But the event which suddenly overwhelmed both of them was violent and unexpected.

In the early morning hours of July 28, 1870, Washington Nathan returned to his home at 12 West Twenty-third Street, New York City, after attending a late supper. As he entered the brownstone, located directly opposite the Fifth Avenue Hotel in one of Manhattan's most prominent areas, Washington called to his father, Benjamin, but his father's bedroom door was shut.

Washington Nathan proceeded to his own room and slept.

At 6:00 A.M., when Washington Nathan awoke, he entered his father's bedroom to arouse him. What he found was a heartbreaking scene of savagery and bloodshed.

There was blood on the floor, on the walls, and all over the bedsheets. Benjamin Nathan had been beaten to death with an instrument, half hammer, half pick, known as a ship carpenter's "dog."

Every major New York newspaper carried the story in headlines on its front page. It described Benjamin Nathan as a prosperous, fine-looking man, fifty-seven, who was noted for his generosity. One of the directors of Mount Sinai Hospital, he had contributed $60,000 to the hospital only three weeks previously. Benjamin Nathan had been a member of the New York Stock Exchange for thirty-four years and his father had been one of its founders. Washington Nathan and his brother Frederick offered a $10,000 reward for information leading to the killer.

The *New York Tribune* reported: "The intense excitement of the Stock Exchange has never been exceeded probably by any event in its history. . . . During the whole day and evening the south steps of the Fifth Avenue Hotel fill with people, gazing at 12 West Twenty-third Street, the scene of the dreadful murder."

But the most disturbing development was the rumor that the prime suspect was the person who discovered the body, Washington Nathan. The police were having difficulty establishing a motive and yet, as the *Tribune* noted, "the insinuation that Washington Nathan was the probable murderer of his father has added to the grief of the family. . . ."

The Stock Exchange closed at 1:00 P.M. on the day of Benjamin Nathan's funeral and New York Mayor A. Oakley Hall offered an additional $5,000 reward for information leading to the murderer's identity.

Washington Nathan was never indicted because of lack of evidence, but due to the scandal, Moses Lazarus forbade Emma to see him again. (Emma had confided her romantic feelings for Nathan to Ralph Waldo Emerson, who on August 19, 1870, wrote her a note of condolence, advising her to keep up her courage.)

Shortly thereafter, Emma wrote a series of autobiographical poems, called *Epochs*, in which her feelings of fruitless love inspired her to create an allegory of despair and the recovery of the human soul.

One of the poems was titled "Lohengrin," who was Parsifal's son and a knight of the Holy Grail in Germanic legend. The poem was dedicated to Washington Nathan.

> The mystic winged and flickering butterfly, A human soul,
> that hovers, giddily

is how Emma pictured man's state, before being overwhelmed by the tragic unexpected—

> —behold! your bolt struck home and over ruined fields the
> storm hath come.

Unable to consummate her relationship with the man she loved, Emma retreated into the closeness of her family, becoming coldly withdrawn and aloof.

She began writing a series of essays for *Century Magazine* on outstanding Jewish figures. It was as if she were attempting to explore her own background. When she admitted that she strongly identified with the poet Heinrich Heine, Emma revealed a great deal about the intellectual conflict within herself. She saw Heine as having "two antagonistic natures" imprisoned in his body—his Jewish compassion and imagination at war with a classic Greek clearness of vision, a pure and healthy love of art for art's sake. She felt that Heine "had preeminently the artistic capacity of playing the spectator to the workings of his own mind. His mordant sarcasm and merciless wit were but the expression of his own sense of the internal incongruity."

But in her analysis of British Prime Minister Benjamin Disraeli she was scathing, as if she were employing a scalpel to cut away the gaudy accompaniments of reputation from her vision of what was true and worthwhile. She identified Disraeli as belonging, along with herself, to the Sephardim of Spanish descent:

> Disraeli was not a first-class man; his qualities were not those of the world's heroes; he possessed talent, rather than genius; he was a sagacious politician aiming at self-aggrandizement, not a wise statesman building his monument in enduring acts of public service; and the study of his career is calculated to dazzle, to entertain, even to amuse, rather than to elevate, to stimulate or to ennoble.

To the world, Jew and non-Jew, she wrote essays in which she presented her analysis of the Jewish people. She made it clear, however, that her interest was in Jewish history, not Jewish theology.

When publisher Philip Cowen of the *American Hebrew Press* challenged a statement she had written as being harmful to orthodox Jews, Emma replied:

> I had not the slightest intention of condemning *all* the orthodox Jews who go to synagogue . . . I only referred in that objectionable phrase to those orthodox Jews whom I classified as clinging to the antiquated ceremonials and repudiating with holy horror the word reform. In my intercourse with Jews I have met several of this class, who

> consider themselves far better Jews than I am and who
> think themselves the props and pillars of Judaism while I,
> on the contrary, think they are its living disgrace.

Backed by Emerson and Whitman, Emma's reputation as a poet
had been steadily growing when the American Committee on the
Statue of Liberty asked her for a sonnet that they might auction
at their Art Loan Exhibition at Twenty-third Street and Fourth
Avenue on December 9, 1883.

Emma's reply was terse: "I am not able to write to order."

By the fall of 1883, the pogroms which had taken place in Russia
forced hundreds of thousands of Jews to flee in order to escape
slaughter. The *London Times* wrote:

> These persecutions, these oppressions, these cruelties,
> these outrages, have taken every form of atrocity in the
> experience of mankind.

A ship arrived in New York with two thousand refugees. They
had been granted temporary quarters at Ward's Island.

With a group of young women, Emma left her family's comfortable new home at 34 East Fifty-seventh Street and traveled by
ferry across the East River to see these poor refugees. It was
November 1, 1883.

The scene on Ward's Island filled Emma with disgust. The
island was covered with refuse. There were no heating facilities,
and the people, dressed in their torn, ragged clothes, were freezing. In the dormitories there were no washing facilities—no fau-
cets, no bathtubs.

Moments after Emma entered the main dormitory, a dozen or
so refugees began shouting that there was not enough food. Suddenly there was a riot as people began running in all directions.
A crowd of police had rushed in and were knocking the refugees
senseless with their clubs.

Leaving the island with her women friends, Emma went directly
to City Hall and demanded to see Mayor Franklin Edson. She
announced to him that she was heading a delegation protesting

the treatment on Ward's Island. Presenting him with a letter describing the conditions that existed, she demanded that something be done immediately. Mayor Edson agreed, after reading the words of Emma's letter—

> ... Not a drop of running water is to be found in dormitories or refectories, or in any of the other buildings, except the kitchen. In all weathers, those who desire to wash their hands or to fetch a cup of water, have to walk over several hundred feet of irregular, dirty ground strewn with rubbish and refuse, and filled, after a rainfall, with stagnant pools of muddy water in which throngs of idle children are allowed to dabble at will . . .

That night Emma returned to Ward's Island. She had anticipated that the victims of the pogroms would be low-class, suitable alms recipients. Instead, as she recalled, "huddled together" in the wooden sheds of the government's unused island, she was amazed to see "men of brilliant talents and accomplishments—the graduates of Russian universities, scholars of Greek as well as Hebrew, and familiar with all the principal European tongues—engaged in menial drudgery, as they defended with zeal the cause of their wretched co-religionists."

She did not always understand what these Jews were saying, but she could see the terrible despair, the fear of death on their faces. They seemed "like people recovered from serious illness—released from a dungeon and finding it impossible to adjust to the new light."

Disturbed—openly and uncontrollably sobbing amidst the hungry, homeless thousands on Ward's Island—this woman who had felt "no religious fervor in my soul" suddenly found herself at one with her people . . .

On November 2, 1883, two days after she had denied their request, the American Committee on the Statue of Liberty received Emma's poem:

THE NEW COLOSSUS

Not like the brazen giant of Greek Fame,
With conquering limbs astride from land to land;

Here at our sea-washed sunset gates shall stand
A mighty woman with a torch, whose flame
Is the imprisoned lightning, and her name
Mother of Exiles. From her beacon-hand
Glows world-wide welcome; her mild eyes command
The air-bridged harbor that twin cities frame.
"Keep, ancient lands, your storied pomp!" cries she
With silent lips. "Give me your tired, your poor,
Your huddled masses yearning to breathe free,
The wretched refuse of your teeming shore.
Send these, the homeless, tempest-tost to me.
I lift my lamp beside the golden door!"

CHAPTER

16

The Gift

THE COBBLESTONE courtyard of 25 rue Chazelles in which the mighty Statue stood was decorated with endless yards of bright red, white, and blue cotton bunting.

Hundreds of French and American flags fluttered from windows of buildings on the adjoining Boulevard de Courcelles and rue Mederic. It was July 4, 1884. All of Paris was aware that the Statue of Liberty was about to be presented as a gift to the United States of America.

As a band played, the United States minister to France, Levi P. Morton, shook hands with the man who had taken the place of Edouard Laboulaye, the new president of the Union Franco-Americaine, Ferdinand de Lesseps.

Lesseps had been a good friend of Laboulaye and, after Laboulaye's death, Bartholdi had asked him to head the committee. At the age of seventy-nine, Lesseps was one of France's most celebrated citizens. For sixty years he had served his nation as a diplomat in Portugal, Africa, Holland, Spain, Egypt . . .

But his crowning achievement had been the financing and construction of the Suez Canal.

White-haired and elegant, Lesseps was known for his great unselfishness and social charm. It was he who, unsuccessfully, had

145

attempted to gain for Auguste the commission to create a light-house for the Suez Canal in 1869.

When the music stopped, the famed diplomat and engineer complimented the creator of the enormous Statue which loomed over Paris. He praised the workers of *Les Compagnons*. The crowd which had jammed into the courtyard intently listened to Lesseps conclude that the Statue was a product of the noblest sentiments which can animate man.

> It is great in its conception and in its realization. It is colossal in its proportions, and we hope that it will grow still greater through its moral value . . . we commit it to your care, Mr. Minister, that it may remain forever the pledge of the bonds which should unite France and the great American nation.

Levi Morton replied by reading a telegram of appreciation from Chester A. Arthur, the president of the United States. He then praised Auguste and those who had worked with him. The band struck up *La Marseillaise* and then *The Star- Spangled Banner*.

Champagne was immediately served in the adjacent offices of Gaget, Gauthier et Cie.

But still there was no pedestal.

A week later, when Joseph Pulitzer arrived in Paris to see the Statue and to meet Auguste Bartholdi, the two men got on won-derfully. As he stood in the courtyard at 25 rue Chazelles, the thirty-six-year-old publisher was enthralled by the wonder that towered above him. Pulitzer and Bartholdi had labored for years to see each of their dreams become real, and Pulitzer could em-pathize with Auguste's struggles.

Later, Pulitzer recalled that Auguste's "smiling face never stopped beaming."

Although Auguste was thrilled to see him, he complained about the progress of the American Committee. In eight years the peo-ple of France had given a total of $400,000 to build the Statue, while the people of America could not raise even one-half of the $225,000 for the Statue's foundation and pedestal. At that rate, the erection of the Statue in New York harbor would not occur until the year 1900.

When Pulitzer left Auguste, he was determined and angry. He promised that he would not stop until the pedestal was a reality.

Work had already begun on Bedloe's Island in New York. The American Committee had named a Civil War veteran, General Charles P. Stone, as chief engineer in charge of constructing a foundation for the pedestal.

What Stone planned to do was to build the foundation directly over the ruins of old Fort Wood. Unfortunately his workmen ran into difficulties when they encountered gigantic slabs of rubble from the foundation of the original fort, which they had to remove.

The cost for the foundation skyrocketed.

Using the remainder of the money that had been raised by the American Committee, Stone's workmen managed to dig an enormous square pit in the center of the fortress and to fill it with a tapering block of concrete fifty-three feet deep, ninety-one feet square at the bottom, and sixty-five feet square at the top.

The foundation was completed in the summer of 1884. An architect had been approached who had agreed to design the pedestal for the Statue. In 1871, during Auguste's first trip to America, at the same dinner party where he had met his future wife, Jeanne-Emilie, John La Farge had introduced him to Richard Morris Hunt. Afterward Auguste noted in his diary: "Met Mr. Hunt, architect from New York, who brags a little, pleased with himself."

Ironically—thirteen years later—this was the architect chosen to create the base for Auguste's masterpiece.

But there was no money for Hunt to begin.

In August 1884, there was a sudden ray of hope.

Supporters of the Statue had successfully lobbied members of the New York State Legislature. The legislature voted to appropriate fifty thousand dollars for the pedestal.

The appropriation was promptly vetoed by New York Governor Grover Cleveland.

CHAPTER

17

Hunt

Hunt was indeed so far above us all in ability, capacity for work, and knowledge, that I cannot imagine any young man who could fail to be rather awe-stricken in his presence. He never did anything by halves; he was the hardest worker I have ever known, and when he played he did it just as energetically, and as earnestly as he worked.

> —FRANK FURNESS, a student of Richard Hunt and founder of the architectural firm of Furness, Evans & Company

ACCOMPANIED BY the strident noises of Manhattan, four lanes of traffic swiftly race down Fifth Avenue past a white, semicircular memorial dedicated to the man who was once America's leading architect.

Located just south of East Seventy-first Street, the memorial is a half-shell ornamented by eight polished marble pillars and two life-sized female figures, one with an anvil and a palette, the other holding the model of a Romanesque temple in her hands.

In the center of the half-shell is the three-foot bronze bust of a robust, middle-aged man.

The man's handsome face has an open, confident expression.

He has a full mustache and beard, a high forehead and direct, watchful eyes. The six-foot stone column which supports his bronze likeness is inscribed:

RICHARD MORRIS HUNT
October 31, 1827
May 31, 1898

In recognition of his services to
the cause of Art in America
this memorial was erected in 1898
by the Art Societies of New York

By the late 1890s, Richard Hunt had become a legend. When it was built, his memorial faced the fairy-tale castles of the rich which he had created up and down Fifth Avenue.

But today he might have been forgotten. For his reputation was never inflated by a sensational murder or a torried love affair, as was that of his contemporary, Stanford White; nor, in fact, do any of Hunt's creations exist today along Fifth Avenue.

Yet he is still remembered by people throughout the world, linked to the vision of Auguste Bartholdi . . . .

In the 1840s Paris was a colorful, exciting place to be an art student and Richard Hunt loved Paris. He admired the contrast between the splendid boulevards and the narrow, ancient streets. He was charmed by the lofty old houses crammed with people from cellar to skylight, which presented, as he recalled, "some attempt at elegance that seemed to make any house in Paris prettier than any house anywhere."

Richard had been born and raised in Brattleboro, Vermont. His father, Jonathan Hunt, was a prominent lawyer, banker and landowner who was elected to the United States House of Representatives in 1827.

After his father's death as a result of a heart attack in 1832, Richard Hunt's mother, Jane, took him to live in Europe. They toured France and Italy, where Richard studied painting. Jane Hunt was herself passionate about art, and she enjoyed sketching. When Richard was eighteen, she encouraged him to study architecture at the Ecole des Beaux Arts in Paris.

Richard was one of the first Americans to be trained at the Ecole. Student life was filled with periods of intense work followed by dinners with wine flowing freely. He met pretty girls, went to the opera, to the theater—or else he frequented the cafes where he could drink, sing, play cards, talk politics until daybreak.

In the 1850s he decided to broaden his knowledge of architecture by seeing as many of the great buildings of the past as he could. Leaving the Ecole, he traveled throughout southern Europe, Egypt, and the Near East, and along the way he studied the palaces of the Doges, the great castles of Germany, the villas of Hadrian and the Borgias, the remains of Egypt's ancient temples, the Parthenon, the Taj Mahal . . .

When Hunt returned to the United States in 1855, at the age of twenty-seven, he was a well-trained, sophisticated man of the world. He was also certain that he was the most knowledgeable architect in America.

But it would take twelve years more before his career flourished.

Using the principles he had learned at the Ecole des Beaux Arts, he began to teach. "Draw, draw, draw, sketch, sketch, sketch!" he would urge his students. "If you can't draw anything else, draw your boots, it doesn't matter, it will ultimately give you a control of your pencil so that you can the more rapidly express on paper your thoughts in designing. The greater facility you have in expressing these thoughts, the freer and better your designs will be."

Five of Hunt's early students were to become prominent architects: Henry Van Brunt, Frank Furness, George Post, William R. Ware, and George Gambrill.

Ware felt that Hunt had an "electric influence" that made his studio "a real home of art, a real fountain of inspiration." Occasionally Hunt would take his students to dinner and the young men would sit, enthralled by his description of his Beaux-Arts days. Ware later said of Hunt's studio: "I think we all of us feel that it was there that we learned all we knew."

In 1866, William Ware established the first professional architectural school in the United States at Massachussets Institute of Technology, and, in 1881, he organized the Department of Architecture at Columbia College in Manhattan. In 1898, Ware wrote that the school at Columbia was a "a direct outcome" of Hunt's studio "thirty-nine years ago."

Frank Furness remembered—

> The first careful drawing in India ink in Mr. Hunt's studio
> was a frightful ordeal. He had such perfect control over
> both his pencil and his brush that it seemed to him im-
> possible that everybody else should not have the same fa-
> cility. The consequence was that the pupil had indeed a
> terrible time, generally ending by Mr. Hunt's snatching the
> brush from his pupil's hand and saying, "There, you clumsy
> idiot, don't you see it is perfectly easy to do? Why don't you
> do it?"

At forty, Hunt had a full head of greying hair, was firmly built
and carried himself with something of a military air. He worked
at his drafting board in shirtsleeves, usually with a black cigar in
his mouth. However, outside his studio he was rigorously correct
in his attire, reluctant to shed his coat and vest until he was confident that there were no ladies present. A man of refined aesthetic
perception, he took great delight in being able to adapt his ideas
to his client's wishes. Eventually, in his commissions for clients of
great wealth, he was able to fulfill their dreams with such inven-
tiveness that he was constantly sought after. In 1871, he built a
mansion for Marshall Field in Chicago, a library at the corner of
Fifth Avenue and East Seventy-first Street in New York City commissioned by philanthropist James Lenox, and Marquand Chapel
at Princeton University.

But 1878 became the turning point of his career. He was introduced to William Kissam Vanderbilt.

None of the Vanderbilts had ever shown a desire to dominate
high society until Cornelius Vanderbilt's grandson, William, married Alva Smith, the daughter of a Mobile, Alabama, cotton
planter. Alva set out to become a lavish hostess and eventually
brought a title into the family by arranging a marriage between
her beautiful daughter, Consuelo, and the ninth Duke of Marl-
borough.

Richard Hunt had newly established his architectural firm at
21 Cortland Street in Manhattan, when William Kissam Vanderbilt, heir to his family's vast railroad empire, asked him to design
and build a mansion for himself and his wife, Alva, on the north-

west corner of Fifth Avenue and Fifty-second Street in New York City.

Vanderbilt had purchased a hundred-foot frontage on the avenue and one hundred and twenty-five feet on Fifty-second Street. His wife Alva's ambition was enormous. "A born dictator," as her daughter Consuelo described her, she made many enemies. She pictured herself living in a French Renaissance chateau in the style of Francis I, from which she could reign as empress of New York society. She repeatedly stipulated to Hunt that the style had to be medieval, "a real Venetian palace like the Doges had."

What Alva and William Vanderbilt wanted was the best money could buy. What Richard Hunt constructed for them was the most remarkable house in New York City.

Hunt covered the mansion with a steeply hipped, blue slate roof, topped by high, ornate copper cresting and massive, richly carved chimney stacks.

Inside the front entrance, the vestibule led into a main hall sixty feet long and twenty feet wide with a beamed and paneled oak ceiling and walls of carved Caen stone, a fine limestone imported from France. Halfway down the hall on the right, opposite a huge stone fireplace, the grand staircase of richly carved Caen stone gave access to the second story. The French Renaissance library with ebony woodwork and the tiled Moorish billiard room were situated on parallel sides of the staircase. Across the main hall was the dark, French walnut-paneled parlor and a white-paneled Regence-Louis XV salon with Boucher tapestries and a Rembrandt portrait.

The most elaborate room in the mansion was the dining room in the rear, fifty feet long by thirty-five feet wide, which rose two stories. Styled in the period of Henry II, the walls were paneled by a seven-foot wainscoting in quartered oak above which tapestries hung over walls faced in Caen stone. At the north end of the room stood huge double fireplaces of red sandstone with caryatids holding the great oak overmantel. At the south end a musician's balcony projected into the hall. On one side, a large, mullioned stained-glass window portrayed the meeting of Francis I and Henry VIII at the Field of the Cloth of Gold.

Richard Hunt's creation contained breakfast rooms decorated with Flemish tapestries, balconied bedrooms, a large gymnasium, and a children's playroom spacious enough to allow the three Vanderbilt children to rollerskate and ride their bicycles.

On the evening of March 26, 1883, a new era was launched in New York society. The Vanderbilts gave a party to show off their new mansion.

"Like an Oriental Dream/The Scene in Mr. W.K. Vanderbilt's Beautiful House Last Evening" was the following morning's headline in the *New York Herald*. The fancy-dress ball had presented a scene "probably never rivaled in republican America and never outdone by the gayest court of Europe," the newspaper article went on.

The party of March 26, 1883, began at 11:00 P.M.

William Kissam Vanderbilt, dressed as the Duc de Guise in a suit of yellow satin, and his wife as a Venetian princess, in cream-colored brocade and heavily bejeweled, greeted their guests on a dias in the French salon.

Cornelius Vanderbilt II came as Louis XVI, while his wife, described as "The Electric Light," appeared in a photograph holding aloft an illuminated orb as if she were imitating the as yet uncompleted Statue of Liberty.

Richard Hunt, clad in knee britches and a mouse-colored hat and cape, elected to pose wryly as Cimabue, the painter whom Dante had chosen to symbolize the transience of fame.

Dancing began at midnight in the guest dining hall. Guests danced quadrille after quadrille, refreshing themselves at intervals by visits to the sumptuous upstairs supper room.

It was noted that over ten thousand flowers were used in Mrs. Vanderbilt's decorations.

The Vanderbilt mansion was such a triumph that almost every millionaire in New York wanted his townhouse and summer cottage designed by Richard Hunt.

And then Hunt was presented with a striking departure. He was approached by Senator William M. Evarts of the American Committee on the Statue of Liberty to design the pedestal which would stand on General Stone's concrete foundation in the middle of New York harbor.

Enthusiastically Hunt agreed.

He had always been a passionate Francophile who strongly believed in the Statue of Liberty's importance. He had designed foundations and impressive settings for statues as part of estates and building facades. But to design the base for the world's most colossal monument was more challenging than any structure he had yet created.

Although the American Committee provided little money, Hunt had begun work by the end of 1883. In his preliminary sketches he drew upon his classical studies. He envisioned the pedestal as a tower which combined the style of the pyramids with the temples designed by the ancient Aztec civilizations. The pedestal would have to be proportionate to the size of the figure placed upon it, yet not so massive or elaborate as to call attention to its presence and turn the viewer's eye from the Statue itself.

Immediately Auguste wrote to him stating that his greatest concern was that the Statue would be positioned securely. He insisted that Hunt obtain competent engineering advice on anchoring the Statue to the pedestal.

Hunt had already met with several engineers. He had also received from Gustave Eiffel, all of Eiffel's drawings and recommendations.

Eiffel had designed and constructed the supporting frame for the Statue—four huge steel girders forming a square—which would be built into the pedestal. Another identical steel square would be built into the pedestal's walls fifty feet below. The two squares would be united by four more enormous iron beams, which would anchor the framework of the Statue itself. Within Hunt's pedestal, Eiffel's steel girders would sink down several stories beneath the Statue's feet.

In the center of the pedestal surrounded by Eiffel's steel squares would be a vertical shaft in which stairways and an elevator would run up into the Statue.

Hunt's first drawings, which he submitted to Bartholdi, pictured the pedestal standing 114 feet high. He called his design Pharos I. With his flare for the classic and historical, Hunt named it after a legendary island lighthouse in the bay of Alexandria.

When the American Committee on the Statue of Liberty complained about the height of the pedestal and its cost, Hunt not only reduced the pedestal's height to eighty-nine feet, but reworked the design, which he submitted to Auguste, calling it Pharos II.

In February 1884, Auguste wrote to Richard Butler:

> I have recently written Hunt about the pedestal of which
> he has forwarded to me a new design which I consider to
> be far inferior to the first. His first design is very good and
> I advised him to keep as much as feasible its general char-
> acter.

Auguste concluded his letter with the one issue which remained
unresolved:

> Let us hope that the patriotic spirit of America will awaken
> and that funds will be coming in . . .

But funds did not come in.

By August 1884, an agreement was made with a quarry in Leete,
Connecticut, to supply white granite for the pedestal. The first
stone was laid on August 5, 1884, after which labor on the pedestal
continued slowly.

On November 10, 1884, work finally had to be shut down. The
American Committee on the Statue of Liberty had exhausted its
efforts. There was no more money.

Richard Hunt sought donations from his patrons. He called on
the August Belmonts, the Astors, the Goelets. Finally, he went to
William K. Vanderbilt, for whom he had built the most magnificent townhouse in Manhattan.

Vanderbilt, like all the others, refused to help.

CHAPTER

18

The Isère

THE PEOPLE of France did not want the Statue to leave. For three years they had watched it grow until it towered over the roofs of the buildings along the boulevards leading to the Arc de Triomphe, the Grand Opera House and the Madeleine. It was their Statue. They had paid four hundred thousand dollars for its construction.

When stories appeared in the French newspapers that the people of the United States could not even raise the funds for a pedestal, many Parisians were indignant. Even though Senator Laboulaye had desired that the Statue should be a gift from France to the people of America, a clamor arose to keep the Statue in Paris.

To resolve the problem, the American minister to France, Levi Morton, with Bartholdi's assistance, promised to build an identical miniature of the Statue of Liberty, paid for by the American residents of Paris. This Statue would be one-fourth the size of the actual Statue of Liberty.*

Auguste had originally announced that the disassembling of the Statue of Liberty for shipment to the United States would begin

---

*Today, this exact miniature of the Statue of Liberty, a gift from the American residents of Paris to the French people, stands overlooking the Seine on the Bridge of Grenelle downstream from the Eiffel Tower.

on August 20, 1884. But, because there was no pedestal, he postponed his plan indefinitely.

A year earlier he had written to Richard Butler:

> All is in good shape . . . but we do not urge on the work, having ample time before us.

By November of 1884, even though three hundred thousand admiring sightseers had been drawn to see the Statue rising from the courtyard of 25 rue de Chazelles, the absence of a pedestal had badly shaken Auguste's hopes.

On November 29, 1884, the constant stream of visitors was joined by an eighty-two-year-old man with white hair, a white beard and a white mustache. Aged and ailing, he was the most revered Frenchman of his time. He had robust, deeply lined cheeks and his puffy eyes were arched and penetrating like the eyes of the gargoyles he had once described on the roof of Notre Dame Cathedral. Victor Hugo was accompanied by his granddaughter, Jeanne, whom he had often pictured in his poems, in addition to several friends.

Auguste's mother was there, as was Jeanne-Emilie.

Hugo kissed Charlotte's hand.

He then entered a room decorated with French and American flags near the base of the Statue. Wearing a loose-fitting jacket, with a white shirt open at the collar, the world famous writer walked hatless in front of the craftsmen of *Les Compagnons*. The workers formed a cluster around him as he reached the entrance to the Statue. "It is superb!" Hugo exclaimed as he examined a diorama showing how the Statue of Liberty would look in New York harbor.

Hugo stopped to talk with Auguste. For several minutes they discussed their mutual friend, Laboulaye, and how sad it was that he had died before seeing the Statue completed.

At that moment, eighty-two-year-old Victor Hugo, frail though he was, suddenly decided that he wanted to climb the 154 steps to the top of the Statue of Liberty.

It took his crowd of friends to stop him.

Before leaving, the writer remained silent for a moment, looking up at the Statue. Finally he murmured:

Yes—this beautiful work aims at what I have always loved—desired—peace between America and France—France which is Europe—this pledge of peace will be permanent. It was a good thing that this should have been done.

Six months later Hugo wrote an inspiration for a pamphlet that would accompany the Statue to America. He was dead within a week, his body placed beneath the Arc de Triomphe in a coffin palled with black and silver and royal purple.

The last published words Victor Hugo ever wrote were treasured by Bartholdi to the end of his life . . .

To Mr. Bartholdi, May 13, 1885
Form to the sculptor is all and yet nothing. It is nothing without the spirit: with the idea it is everything.

Victor Hugo

Although work on the pedestal was still shut down in America, in 1885, Bartholdi closed the Statue to the French public so that it could be disassembled. The task was enormous. Each of the parts had to be numbered and crated.

Auguste was plunged into even deeper gloom by an article which appeared in the *New York Times*:

The painful parsimony of the Frenchmen who have undertaken to present this city with the Statue of "Liberty Enlightening the World" is simply disgusting. They have,

in effect, told us that we cannot have the Statue unless we
provide it with a pedestal. This effort to compel us to pay
out of our own money for the embellishment of our harbor
has not yet been condemned by the press with the severity
it deserves.

The article then suggested that the French erect the Statue
themselves and pay ten thousand dollars a year as rent for the
site.

Resistance to the financing of the pedestal became so pervasive
that the American Committee on the Statue of Liberty was forced
to concede its failure to raise more funds. In March 1885, with
Richard Hunt's work on the pedestal at a standstill, a letter signed
by William Evarts, Richard Butler, and Henry Spaulding finally
admitted the pathetic truth:

If the money is not forthcoming the Statue must return to
its donors to the everlasting disgrace of the American people, or it must go to some other city to the everlasting
disgrace of New York.

Joseph Pulitzer had remarked to Richard Butler in a letter on
January 12, 1885: "Of course you know that I will do everything
I can to finish the pedestal."

By now he was a pioneer of a bold, innovative style of newspaper
publishing never before known in New York City.

Into this city, five hundred thousand immigrants poured an-
nually, many remaining in ghettos below Union Square. By 1885,
Manhattan housed the most brutal, teeming squalor in the world,
worse than London or Bombay. Starving women and children
toiled twelve hours a day for fifty cents or less, and tuberculosis
was rampant. Nowhere on earth could compare with the extremes
of wealth and poverty found on Fifth Avenue, from the Louis XV
chateaux and Venetian palazzos constructed by Richard Hunt to
the abysmal filth and deprivation of Mulberry Bend situated on
the Lower East Side.

Pulitzer's *World* was the first newspaper to reveal the existing
horrors. It attacked the wealthy robber barons for exploiting the
helplessness of the poor. Depicting the poor at Christmas without
bread, much less turkey and plum pudding, the *World* charged:

Take a lot 25 feet front and 100 feet deep, and erect a building 25 by 80 on it, with accommodations for four families on each of its five or six floors, and you are simply making a trap to smother people.

The *World* told the story of Kate Sweeny:

She had lain down in the cellar to sleep, and the sewer that runs under the house overflowed and suffocated her where she lay. No one will ever know who killed Kate Sweeny. No one will ever summon the sanitary inspectors. . . . Nobody seems to have thought it worth an investigation.

Pulitzer assailed the greed which prevailed over human decency—the lust for Newport palaces and pet animals with diamond collars, the rush to marry foreign titles. He editorialized:

Take it altogether, some of our good society, when measured by the demands of the community in which it lives, is a very selfish and barren society.

The *World* became the voice of the common man—a voice which seldom had been heard in American journalism. It exposed how the government, which derived most of its income from taxing real estate, shifted the tax onto the poor in the form of high rents. "Wealth escapes taxation!" The *World* exclaimed, revealing how William H. Vanderbilt, the father of William Kissam Vanderbilt, with a fortune estimated at $200 million, had avoided taxation by swearing that his debts exceeded his income. Telegraph and transit tycoon Cyrus Field had done the same.

Pulitzer was neither a socialist nor an anarchist. He insisted that enlightened capitalism was the great hope of democracy. But he was fearful that greed and the excesses of extravagance would incite a bitter struggle between the rich and the poor:

We respect wealth when it is made the instrument of good . . . we despise wealth when it is prostituted to shoddy display and the gratification of coarse and vulgar tastes.

By the spring of 1885, the *World* had become one of the most controversial newspapers in New York. Pulitzer was cursed at the Union League Club and praised by common workmen who could not spell his name.

Within two years, the *World's* daily circulation had grown from twenty thousand to one hundred thirty-five thousand.

But the unassembled goddess of Liberty waiting in humiliation in France preyed on Pulitzer's mind. Vilified by such papers as the *Herald* and the *New York Times,* shunned by New York's rich, and failed by the American Committee, the Statue of Liberty faced disaster. On March 16, 1885, angrily challenging the indifference and animosity of New York's citizenry, Pulitzer made his famous appeal:

> Money must be raised to complete the pedestal for the Bartholdi Statue. It would be an ineffaceable disgrace to New York City and the American Republic to have France send this splendid gift without our having provided even so much as a landing place for it . . . there is but one thing that can be done. We must raise the money . . . the two hundred and fifty thousand dollars* that the making of the Statue cost was paid in by the masses of the French people—by the working men, the tradesmen, the shopgirls, the artisans—by all, irrespective of class or condition. Let us respond in like manner. Let us not wait for the millionaires to give the money. . . . Take this appeal to yourself personally. It is meant for every reader of THE WORLD. Give something, however little. Send it to us.

Pulitzer's editorial ended with the promise:

> We will publish the name of every giver, however small the sum given. Let us hear from the people.

Slowly subscriptions began to come in.

The Hotel Men's Relief Society donated $232. Pulitzer responded by printing the names of every hotel man who donated, as well as the names of their hotels, along with the letter accompanying the check. To Pulitzer, no donation was too small. And

---

*The actual amount finally to complete the Statue was $400,000.

he kept his promise to publish the name of every contributor, no matter the size of the contribution.

A five-year-old boy from Astoria, Queens, affected by a drawing the *World* printed picturing Uncle Sam holding his hat outstretched beside the globe of the world, wrote: "Please put enclosed (60 cents) onto the old man's hat, for I love him too much to see him beg."

By March 19, three days after Pulitzer's editorial—"Let us not wait for the millionaires"—the *World* had raised $813.21. Everywhere readers were moved by the messages which Pulitzer printed:

> I am a poor man or I would send more than the enclosed 10 cents for the Liberty fund. There's lots of we un's who have been reading the *Herald* for years and who are now buying a paper called the *World*. You go right on Mr. World and make it red hot for all the nobs and snobs.
>
> Respectfully yours,
> E. James

> D. Greenwood, D. Thomas, 1 cent each; Frank Huff, George Friff, Ethel Nixon, 1 cent each; Cora Colbert, 5 cents; Willie Smith, 2 cents; May Stern and Horace Stone, 2 cents each. . . .

Curious crowds had been turned away from the gates of 25 rue de Chazelles in Paris as stories reached newspapers everywhere: The Statue of Liberty had been dismantled. Its copper and iron components had been numbered. Packed in 210 wooden cases, which varied in weight between 150 pounds and three tons, the colossal figure was transported through the city by horsedrawn wagons to the Gare St. Lazare, where it was loaded onto seventy railroad trucks.

The process of loading and the trip from Paris to the north of France took seventeen days.

At the seaport of Rouen in northern France, the 210 wooden cases were unloaded from the seventy railroad trucks and taken on board a vessel—the three-masted French warship *Isère*—under orders of Jules Grevy, president of the French Republic. It was common for the French to name their battleships after French provinces, such as Moselle, Lyonnais and Le Bourgogne. Isére was a district in southeast France bordering the Swiss Alps.

On a cloudy spring day, May 21, 1885, the *Isère* sailed from Rouen, bound for New York harbor.

Pulitzer's attacks were relentless. He announced that the *World* had received a joint donation from William H. Vanderbilt and Jay Gould amounting to four hundred dollars, *in Confederate money*. He reminded his readers that the German people had raised $750,000 for Bismarck's seventieth birthday, whereas Americans could not part with one-third of that sum for Liberty.

No other New York newspaper joined to help the *World,* but as donations poured in and Pulitzer continued to print the name of each giver and the amount daily, newspapers all over America suddenly announced their support.

The *Pittsburgh Post* encouraged: "The *World* is getting along splendidly with the Bartholdi Festival. We watch its progress with great interest. Not a word of encouragement does it get from the other New York papers. A tinge of jealousy here?"

The *Boston Transcript* noted, "It is a gratifying fact that the popular subscriptions in New York for the erection of the Bartholdi Statue average about $1.25 each. If working men can give $1.25, surely Vanderbilt and Gould will feel justified in putting out $4 or $5, even in these times of depression."

The *Rochester Post-Express* praised the *World's* efforts, but added, "The French frigate *Isère* has left Rouen for New York with Bartholdi's Statue of Liberty Enlightening the World. It would be a national disgrace if the pedestal were not ready by the time the Statue arrives."

But there were still not enough funds for Richard Hunt to resume work on the pedestal.

The columns of the *World* began to swell with the names of people sending in money, expanding each day, from four columns, to six, to eight. Pulitzer, in his editorials, praised the groups uniting to raise funds—"the shop-girls are throwing in their dimes and quarters. They are doing just what the shop-girls of Paris did when the money was needed for Bartholdi's great Statue." He praised the carpet dealers of New York and Brooklyn, the employees of the National Express Company, the agents of the Knickerbocker Ice Company. It was as if the pedestal had become a prime concern of working people everywhere. Passionately, the thirty-eight-year-old publisher exulted—

> There is a great common heart in this country that is generous and patriotic. It needs only to be awakened. That awakening is now taking place, and, mark the prediction— when Bartholdi comes here with his splendid Goddess of Liberty, he will be welcomed with such a warm outburst of enthusiasm as will reach over the seas to France and tell the people of our sister Republic that Americans are neither discourteous nor ungrateful.

By June 1, the *Isère* was almost halfway to America.

Then a violent North Atlantic storm erupted and the vessel with its 225,000-pound cargo was mercilessly buffeted by gale winds for days. Sixty-foot waves drove it off course.

America anxiously waited for news of the ship's safety.

The *World* received a check for $16.88 from Rabbi F. de Sola Mendes of the synagogue located at West Forty-fourth Street and Sixth Avenue, New York City. The money had been raised from the children's classes.

Mr. J.C. Fargo, president of the Wells Fargo Company, sent in a substantial contribution from 1,200 subscribers and employees of Wells Fargo throughout the country.

A sum of $606 arrived from members of the watch and jewelry trade. Each member had donated a dollar and members' names filled a twenty-five foot scroll. The *World* managed to squeeze all the names, four abreast, into a single column.

Frank Siddall of Philadelphia began sending in one dollar a day, promising to continue until the pedestal was paid for. Mr. C.C. Shayne of 103 Prince Street donated a sealskin dolman valued at $600. Mr. Pierre Lorillard, a descendant of the founder of America's oldest tobacco company, gave $1,000 in cash. Money came in postal orders, gold, stamps, nickels, dimes, pennies, bills, and silver dollars.

By the first week of June, response to Pulitzer's appeal totaled more than fifty thousand dollars.

The *Isère* arrived on June 17, 1885.

The French North Atlantic Squadron, commanded by Admiral Phillippe Lacombre, intercepted the three-masted warship and led her into New York harbor in triumph.

Amidst hundreds of flags flying blue, white, and red colors, the captain of the *Isère,* Commandant Louis de Saune, formally presented the 210 wooden cases containing the pieces of the Statue of Liberty to General Charles P. Stone, who had built the foundation and was in charge of construction on Bedloe's Island.

The *Isère,* with the 210 marked cases in its hold, docked off Sandy Hook, New Jersey, as Pulitzer stepped up his attempts to raise money for the pedestal.

> Editor of the *World*—
> We are four little boys—we *were* seven—but Frankie, Herbie and Dougie wanted their money for fire-crackers. We know that the "glorious Fourth" would more "terrible burn" next year if "Liberty's pure beacon glowed." So we have given our $3 to you. Please put our names in your paper. They are Sammy, Bobbie, Genie and Little Charlie.

On June 6, 1885, *Harper's Weekly* published an article stating that the pedestal had already been completed inside the stone walls of Bedloe's Island and "was worthy of the great figure which would stand on it."

In truth, there was no pedestal, and the unpacked cases aboard the *Isère* prompted Pulitzer to try to locate the balance of the $100,000 needed as quickly as possible. Continuing to criticize the rich, he announced on June 19 that $74,183.46 had been raised. His attempt to find 100 contributors who would give $250 each failed. For the most part, money kept arriving in small amounts.

By July 3, 1885, the *World* had printed the names of 100,000 contributors.

On July 4, $26 was received from Mabel Chase, treasurer of the Irving Club at Franklin, Essex County, New Jersey, from a lawn party given for the benefit of the fund. From Bangor, Maine, W.S. Hazeltine and James T. Slater both gave $1. From Tillie Bloom and Fredie Frye was received 2 cents each, and from Charles Kithehart, Lizzie Leary, and Nicholes Hager, 3 cents each.

On July 7, Pulitzer announced that $90,000 had been raised. The wooden cases containing the Statue were being unloaded. Richard Hunt resumed work on the pedestal. The residents of the Chelsea Hotel, located at 220 West Twenty-third Street, Manhattan, donated $8.25; Jere Wernberg, a Brooklyn attorney, gave $50, Louise M. Fulton, C.H. Lane, and D.M. Holdridge contributed $1 each. . . .

The great announcement came on August 11, 1885. The *World* proclaimed in a headline across its front page:

ONE HUNDRED THOUSAND DOLLARS
TRIUMPHANT COMPLETION OF THE
WORLD'S FUND FOR THE LIBERTY PEDESTAL

The funds had been raised in five months from over 120,000 people. On the last day, money had to be turned away. The final donation, $250, had been donated by inventor Thomas Alva Edison.

CHAPTER
19

The Unveiling

AT FIRST all agreed to have the Statue of Liberty unveiled in the late summer of 1886. But on April 16, 1886, Bartholdi, remembering the Philadelphia Exposition of 1876 and the illness he had suffered because of the intense hot weather, wrote to Richard Butler to reset the date:

> The Fall is the season when we have the people in the City, or close to it, and the weather is more pleasant than the summer . . . it would be well to try to have the American government invite the French to send some representatives. I shall proceed to do the same here. We must not forget that Diplomatic people are very slow moving.

On April 18, 1886, a concerned Auguste Bartholdi again wrote to Richard Butler:

> I hope that everything is going well with the mounting of the Statue.

Finally, the date for the unveiling was agreed upon: October 28, 1886.

Because of his work on the Eiffel Tower, already rising on the

Champs de Mars in Paris, Gustave Eiffel had not come to New York to supervise the erection of the Statue's iron skeleton. However, his instructions were so precise that Richard Hunt and General Stone were able to supervise its growth out of the center of Hunt's pedestal.

Richard Hunt's pedestal had taken eight months to complete. The American Committee had finally approved his first design, Pharos I, with the modifications that he reduce the height and that he redesign the upper part, which had been a solid mass rising from the base.

The final pedestal stood eighty-nine feet and the solid mass of the top had been transformed into a gallery with Doric columns with varied and intricate designs across its granite face.

Fears that the Statue would fall off its pedestal into the harbor were silenced by the genius of Eiffel's construction. The eight steel girders which had been planted horizontally within the pedestal were securely connected to the iron beams which traveled up into the Statue's skeleton.

On July 12, 1886, a ceremony was held on Bedloe's Island. Workmen dangling from scaffolds began hammering the 600,000 rivets which would bind Liberty's 300 pieces of copper skin to its iron skeleton.

The initial sheet of copper was placed near Liberty's right heel.

The first rivet was engraved with the name Bartholdi—the second, Pulitzer—the third, Eiffel—the fourth, Hunt. . . .

New York wanted the celebration to take place on October 28, 1886. For Auguste, it would be the final realization of his hopes and labors—but his moment of glory once again seemed fated to be doomed. Early in October, eighty-five-year-old Charlotte Bartholdi became critically ill.

Torn between his feelings for his mother and his desire to go to New York to see his Statue unveiled, Auguste wrote to Richard Butler on October 8:

> I am in a very painful situation. I do not know whether I shall be able to come or not. My mother is sick, I do not know exactly how serious is the illness, but I am sure she

needs care. I would be very sorry, dear friend, to lose this opportunity to enjoy with you the fulfilling of all our hopes, and the ending of all our troubles.

20

October 28, 1886

EXCITEMENT BEGAN to build from the moment the steamship *La Bretagne* was sighted off Fire Island at 5:00 P.M. on Sunday, October 24, 1886. The French vessel had to be quarantined before entering New York harbor.

Reporters from the *New York Tribune*, the *New York Herald* and the *World* attempted to board the ship, but the seas were too rough. Bartholdi appeared on deck, wearing a tight-fitting blue naval cap. Charlotte Bartholdi, although gravely ill, had insisted that he and Jeanne-Emilie travel to New York for the unveiling of his Statue. The reporter from the *World* sent Auguste a note of welcome with Joseph Pulitzer's compliments.

The reporters from the three New York newspapers noted that Auguste was soon joined on deck by eighty-two-year-old Ferdinand de Lesseps. The famed builder of the Suez Canal wore a heavy overcoat and Scotch cap. Only a little of his face and grey mustache could be seen. Lesseps was accompanied by his eight-year-old daughter, Tototte, who had been sick during the entire ten-day voyage from Le Havre.

The steamship *La Bretagne* remained in quarantine overnight.

The following morning at eight, in a heavy fog, the yacht *Tillie* steamed out to meet the French vessel. Joseph Pulitzer, one of the

173

most successful publishers in New York, whose paper's circulation during the twenty-one-week campaign to raise money for the pedestal had risen from 130,000 to 235,000, helped the radiant Jeanne Bartholdi aboard the boat, giving her his arm. The chic Jeanne-Emilie wore an elegantly fitting dress of navy blue serge, a sealskin sacque, and a felt hat with a graceful wing of green and black feathers.

Pulitzer embraced Bartholdi and Lesseps.

On board the *Tillie*, Auguste was warmly greeted by Richard Hunt, Senator William Evarts and his daughter, Marie Glaenzer. Auguste had never seen his Statue assembled in New York harbor—standing as proudly as he had pictured it in his vision.

Through the dense fog the steamship chugged toward Bedloe's Island. But soon they feared that they would be disappointed. It was too dark to see. The sky was black with clouds.

And then the clouds lifted.

Bartholdi hurried to the rail. The sun shone on the Statue of Liberty, which, Senator Evarts later described, was "glistening like gold." Jeanne Bartholdi, eyes filled with tears, pressed the hand of Marie Glaenzer and exclaimed, "How beautiful!"

Looking up, Bartholdi saw it for the first time—the realization of his dream. "I feel happiness," he murmured. "Perfect happiness."

Landing on Bedloe's Island, Auguste complimented Richard Hunt on the grace of his pedestal. Tapping one of the pedestal's corners, he remarked, "I have always liked this Egyptian style. I hope that this base will last as long as the pyramids along the Nile."

Lesseps had come ashore holding his hat in his hands. He was overwhelmed by the presence of the Statue. "It has surpassed my expectations. I was prepared for a great work of art, but this is sublime. It is simply faultless."

Meanwhile, Tototte had sprung to life, running around the island, disappearing in and out of the Statue's base as she played with a small chunk of granite from the pedestal.

The visitors from France were then taken back on board the yacht to the fresh, green park at the edge of Manhattan and finally, in carriages, to the warm, comfortable Hoffman House, a hotel on Broadway between Twenty-fourth and Twenty-fifth

Streets. Bartholdi was officially received by Mayor William R. Grace, who presented him with a parchment granting him the Freedom of, the City. Wherever he went choirs sang the *Marseillaise*. At the Union League Club of New York, he was received by J. Pierpont Morgan, Theodore Roosevelt, and the statesman, Elihu Root—all in preparation for the great day to come. . . .

The celebration honoring the Statue of Liberty began exactly one hundred feet from the front door of 34 East Fifty-seventh Street, where Emma Lazarus lived with her four sisters.

But Emma was not to take part in the festivities. After her unfortunate involvement with Washington Nathan, she had taken refuge within her family.

A desperate vacuum was created in her life by her mother's death in 1883 and she became emotionally dependent upon her father, Moses.

When Moses Lazarus died on March 9, 1885, her sister Josephine remembered: "It was a crushing blow for Emma . . . Life lost all its meaning and charm."

Grief-stricken and suffering from an illness the doctors could not diagnose, Emma sailed for Europe on August 14, 1885.

She had not returned.

At 9:00 A.M. on Thursday, October 28, 1886, General Charles Stone, the grand marshal who had supervised the work on Bedloe's Island, appeared on a black horse at the intersection of Fifty-seventh Street and Fifth Avenue. It was a wet, raw New York day and the five-mile route down Fifth Avenue was already a vast sea of soggy bunting and French tricolors. American stars and stripes hung from doorways and roof-tops as over a million people elbowed against each other to watch the biggest parade in the city's history.

At every corner were carts selling souvenirs. At the corner of Fifty-fifth Street and Fifth Avenue, a man dressed as Auguste Bartholdi sold commemorative copper medals embossed with the Statue of Liberty on one side and Bartholdi's likeness on the other. Photographs and drawings of him were peddled by the thousands. Even pictures of the Brooklyn Bridge were hawked at one cent apiece. Newly arrived Italian immigrants were told that it too was Auguste's work.

A force of 250 policemen was positioned to keep order, in addition to 100 detectives assigned to circulate with the crowds. News had reached the city that thieves were traveling from all parts of the country to descend on New York.

Mayor Grace had shut down all city offices and issued a proclamation recommending that proprietors close their shops during the parade. The parade was scheduled to move down Fifth Avenue to Washington Square, then to Broadway, and down Broadway to the Battery. According to the *New York Herald,* the beflagging of the city along the parade route had begun very early. "I am selling so many French flags that I am forgetting my English," a Fulton Street flag dealer reportedly remarked. Families came on ferries from Brooklyn carrying wooden boxes to stand on. Others arrived on horseback.

With General Stone in the lead, the procession slowly moved down Fifth Avenue, passing St. Thomas Episcopal Church at Fifty-third Street, the mansion Richard Hunt had splendidly designed for William K. Vanderbilt at Fifty-second Street, and St. Patrick's Cathedral at Fiftieth Street. Near the Windsor, Hawk, Waite and Wetherbee Hotel at Forty-seventh Street, there was a deafening sound that echoed for blocks—a thousand horses neighing and pawing the ground insistently, awaiting some of the parade's missing participants.

The first division of the parade was the Seventh Regiment. Crowds cheered as it passed the Fifth Avenue Baptist Church at Forty-sixth Street, Dr. Chapin's Universalist Church at Forty-fifth Street, and Temple Emanuel with its elaborate Moorish design at Forty-third Street.

Crossing Forty-second Street, the marchers paraded by the enormous two-square-block Croton Reservoir, located directly across Fifth Avenue from Rutgers Female College. They marched by the Union League Club at Thirty-ninth and continued along the brownstone-lined avenue past the New York Aquarium on Thirty-fifth Street.

Below this street where numerous buildings were being demolished, masses of spectators had climbed onto the scaffolding to watch the parade go by. Thousands of people stood on heaps of stones torn from the surface of Fifth Avenue for repaving. Seats on horse cars standing on Twenty-fifth Street rented for fifty cents.

The parade passed near the empty Broadway Theater on Thirtieth Street, Dr. Ormiston's Dutch Reformed Church on Twenty-ninth Street, the Fifth Avenue Theater, where Lilly Langtry was performing in *The Lady of Lyons* at Twenty-eighth Street, eventually reaching the Fifth Avenue Hotel at Twenty-fourth Street . . .

In the Madison Square reviewing stand at Twenty-third Street and Fifth Avenue, world leaders vied with the very rich for seats of prominence. As the Seventh Regiment Band approached, it began playing the *Marseillaise.* In front of the receiving stand marched volunteer firemen, policemen, fraternal organizations, veterans of the Grand Army of the Republic, the Grenadiers Rochambeau, the Société Israelite, the Garde Lafayette, and bands of every description. One hundred carriages held members of the Aztec Society, composed of veteran officers who had fought in the war with Mexico. There were George Washington's carriage pulled by eight white horses, carriages carrying judges and governors, mayors from various cities, school groups, patriotic societies—it seemed as if America had finally gone crazy over the Statue of Liberty.

Nearly every resident of the city who was not watching the parade was marching through the rain. As band after band and unit after unit marched down Fifth Avenue past Lord and Taylor at Nineteenth Street, Arnold Constable at Eighteenth Street, and Tiffany and Company at Fourteenth Street, the thousands took so long to pass the Madison Square reviewing stand that Mayor Grace's official luncheon had to be canceled so that dignitaries could scurry over to the Hudson River.

At 1:00 P.M. there was a naval procession of the Atlantic Squadron through the harbor, led by the flagship *Tennessee.* Around the mighty ships gathered tiny boats, little sail craft, superb private yachts, huge-tonnage merchant steamers, and thundering ironclads, side by side with pleasure craft of every name and little screaming tugs sending forth their shrill signals. Bands blared, whistles blasted, and guns boomed.

"New York," reported the *World*, "was one vast cheer."

But the rain kept falling.

While the gigantic naval flotilla cruised through New York harbor, the marchers and floats were still making their way along Broadway. But soon, anxious spectators began leaving the line of march to hurry down to the Battery. There, hundreds of thousands were already densely jammed, waiting.

They could not see. Through the rain they could only dimly make out the majestic image in the distance—the tallest structure in the world—standing over three hundred feet tall against the dark sky.

It seemed ironic that so many of the people who huddled, cramped together in the rain at the southern tip of Manhattan, were those who had paid for the foundation and the pedestal, while, amidst the popping of champagne corks, the offical boats going out to Bedloe's Island were filled with the rich who had given nothing, but had used their influence to be in the official party.

As he waited impatiently inside the head of his Statue to loosen her unveiling cord, Auguste looked down through the ten-foot diadem windows overlooking the great harbor. The vision he had lived with since he was a young man was about to come true. It had cost him a fortune. It had taken fifteen years of his life.

But Auguste's passion for his dream had forced him onward, never allowing him to forget that summer morning, years before, when he first entered that same harbor and envisioned a Statue that would stand forever.

Just as all the avenues of Paris led to the gleaming Arc de Triomphe, built before he was born, all the people he had met had, like those avenues, led him to this moment—Edouard de Laboulaye, Victor Hugo, Gustave Eiffel, John La Farge, Charles Gounod, Joseph Pulitzer.

The Statue of Liberty would make the name Auguste Bartholdi world famous. He was only seconds away from its unveiling.

When the three-hundred-pound figure of the president of the United States, Grover Cleveland, stepped on the shore of Bedloe's Island, with his black mustache and red cheeks, carrying a russet bag in his hand and wearing a silk hat, there was an ear-shattering twenty-one-gun salute. The smoke from the guns rose, mingling with the rain and thick fog, so that Bartholdi could no longer make out what was happening.

He was to pull the cord releasing the veil at a signal from a boy on the ground three hundred feet below.

But he could no longer see the boy.

At the foot of the Statue, there were American and French flags everywhere. Above the speaker's platform was a banner inscribed with the words:

A. BARTHOLDI—LIBERTY

Except for Jeanne-Emilie and Lesseps' daughter, Tototte, women were excluded from attending the unveiling ceremony. The official reason given was that they might get hurt in the crowd, but the real reason was that women were generally excluded from public ceremonies.

It was a man's world.

In anger, Mrs. Lillie Devereux Blake, president of the New York State Suffrage Association, called on "all persons interested in securing political Liberty for women" to join her. She had chartered a boat and loaded it with several hundred women. They ordered the boat's captain to sail as close to Bedloe's Island as possible.

As the head of the American Committee, Senator William M. Evarts, rose to introduce the president of the United States, the boat filled with women drew near. There was unexpected pandemonium when tiny, brown-haired Mrs. Blake, who seemed to have a more powerful voice than any man present, interrupted Senator Evart's speech. Loudly she cried out praising the embodiment of Liberty as woman—and then in a stirring appeal added how despicable it was that, should Liberty came to sudden life, she would not be allowed to vote either in France or the United States.

At that moment, a cannon mistakenly went off and Bartholdi tugged the unveiling cord. The great tricolor fell aside.

The ships around the island began to blast whistles. Guns roared in salute.

The defeated Senator Evarts sat down, his hands over his eyes in despair.

Bands began to play. People cheered.

And then Grover Cleveland, who only two years before as governor of the state of New York had defeated an appropriation bill to finance the pedestal, rose and addressed the crowd as he accepted the monument on the part of the United States of America.

If his words seemed out of character, they at least reflected the feelings of those who had struggled and gone before him:

> We will not forget that Liberty has made here her home, nor shall her chosen altar be neglected. Willing votaries will constantly keep alive its fires and these shall gleam upon the shores of our sister Republic in the East. Reflected thence and joined with answering rays, a stream of light shall pierce the darkness of ignorance and men's oppression until Liberty enlightens the world.

There were cries for Bartholdi to speak, but they were silenced by the master of ceremonies, Major General Richard Scholfield, who, in order to hurry the process, shouted impatiently: "Mr. Bartholdi has nothing to say, so there's no use talking about it."

In fact, Auguste had not yet come down from the crown of the Statue.

There were more speeches, by Ferdinand de Lesseps, French Minister Antoine Lefaivre, the president of the Union League Club, Chauncey Depew, and a final invocation by Reverend Henry C. Potter, an Episcopalian clergyman from New York.

As Bartholdi descended from the Statue, he was warmly greeted by the dignitaries present. It was then that the real trouble began, the unimaginable occurred.

Fireworks filled the sky. The police succeeded in keeping the crowd back so that President Cleveland could board his private launch for his return to New York. But the proceedings had lasted too long, and it was almost dark. The 3,500 people crowded onto the island suddenly became desperate to leave.

As Cleveland's boat left the shore, there was instant panic. People raced in terror toward the pier, afraid of being left to spend the night on the island. The police attempted to intervene, but they were shoved back. The crush was terrible.

In the nightmare that followed, Lesseps' daughter Tototte was knocked down and dragged, screaming. Auguste ran to rescue Jeanne.

One of the French delegates shouted, "This is not merely disgraceful—it is outrageous!" People were running in all directions.

Auguste discovered Cornelius Vanderbilt crouching in one of the narrow passages leading from Fort Wood. He managed to rescue him before he was crushed by the mob. Vanderbilt was bleeding from the nose and mouth.

A reporter from the *New York Daily Tribune* noted that the police present "served rather to ornament the shores of the island than to preserve order."

Auguste located Jeanne and they managed to escape in a small boat moored at the shore.

It took several hours, but finally, in pitch darkness, the island was evacuated.

The party at Delmonico's that evening was one of the most lavish ever given in New York. Hosted by the Chamber of Commerce of New York State, two hundred guests paid tribute to Bartholdi. Beneath the magnificent French crystal chandeliers, an orchestra played until 1:00 A.M.

Auguste Bartholdi, elegantly dressed in white tie and tails, was presented with two elaborate white silk badges which Lafayette had worn on his last visit to America in 1829. Auguste remarked that someone had called him the Columbus of Bedloe's Island because no one had discovered the island before him.

As the evening went on, the speeches and toasts to Liberty became inspiring and passionate. Bathed by the glittering atmosphere, the two hundred guests cheered and applauded as Auguste told them that he was accepting this reception not for himself, but "for my country—for France and for Alsace."

There were more praises, more tributes, more hands to shake, more people congratulating him. The massive president of the United States embraced him. Jovially pounding Bartholdi on the back, Grover Cleveland roared, "You are the greatest man in America today!"

In the early hours of the morning, as Auguste fell asleep in his suite at the Hoffman House, Jeanne-Emilie sat up writing a letter to Charlotte Bartholdi in Colmar:

> Auguste is feeling fine. His dear face is shining with pleasure. What enthusiasm! What a triumph! . . Our dear Auguste has been feted like a monarch. We can be proud: You to be his mother, and I to be his wife. How happy I

am to see Auguste so justly rewarded after so much labor! In one day he saw the whole population hail him; in every mouth was the name Bartholdi.

Epilogue

In a century the centenary of Independence will be celebrated again. We shall then be only forgotten dust. America, who will then have hundreds of millions of inhabitants, will be ignorant of our names. But this Statue will remain . . . the visible proof of our affection . . . it will stand there unshaken in the midst of the winds which will roar around its head and the waves which will shatter their fury at its feet.

—EDOUARD LABOULAYE,
July 4, 1875

IT WAS Auguste Bartholdi's desire that Bedloe's Island would become a kind of Pantheon, that around the Statue of Liberty would be placed the statues of America's noblest leaders, so that the island "should become a sort of pilgrimage."

His wish was never fulfilled.

But in the early 1980s, another sculptor, Phillip Ratner, after soliciting funds from private donors and the United States government, created five cast iron statues which stand in a small garden just north of Richard Hunt's pedestal.

Each statue stands almost four feet tall.

Randomly assembled, as if each figure were on its own amidst the trees and flowers, they touchingly illustrate the birth of the Statue of Liberty.

In the forefront, the scholarly Laboulaye stands, pensively gazing toward the finished monument.

Nearby, Auguste, with one foot resting on his work pedestal, fashions the first clay model of the Statue.

Next to him, Gustave Eiffel holds a model of the Eiffel Tower, gazing at its perfection.

Beside Eiffel, the tall, dignified Joseph Pulitzer, wearing a pince-nez, studies a copy of the *World*.

Finally, near the edge of the garden is the thin, tense figure of Emma Lazarus, holding a volume of her poems.

Emma Lazarus and Joseph Pulitzer never met. Yet no two people in America did more for the Statue.

When the Statue was unveiled in 1886, thirty-seven-year-old Emma Lazarus was already dying. In 1885, after her father's death, when the doctors were not able to diagnose her condition, she had traveled alone to Europe. Once before she had sailed to Europe, in 1873, and had considered it the greatest event of her life. At the time, in the spring of 1875, a great admirer, the novelist Henry James, wrote to her, "I have an idea you will be back in England about this time and am writing you to wait and see when this event occurs."

After spending several months in England, visiting James, attending the theater and the opera, she had gone on to Holland and Italy. In Rome she had been filled "with the excitement of this tremendous place." But she found that Paris had changed—"all the ghosts of the Revolution were gone." At the Louvre, she knelt at the feet of Venus—"the goddess without arms, who cannot help"—and then ill, weak, and racked with pain, she returned home.

Although she passed the newly unveiled colossus in New York harbor, she never wrote of the Statue of Liberty again.

Within six months she was dead.

One year later, in 1888, Joseph Pulitzer sat in his office in the early hours of the morning reading over the galleys of his next edition.

"Would you brighten the lamp?" Pulitzer asked a clerk sitting nearby.

"It's already bright."

"Not for me."

From that day until his death in 1911, Pulitzer lived in darkness, a victim of total blindness.

Before the end, unable to bear living in New York, the publisher decided to spend his remaining years touring the world on his private yacht, which he named after the one accomplishment that had brought him his greatest satisfaction—*Liberty.*

In the summer of 1891, throngs of immigrant families with bright-colored headgear and squalling children poured into New York harbor. Among them was a lost, bewildered twelve-year-old girl. Dark-haired Kathryn Brownly had traveled across the Atlantic alone.

The last six years of Kathryn's life, since her mother's death, had been spent in the town of Clones, in Monahan County, Ireland. Her father had left her there when she was six, to come to America.

Early in 1891, her father had written to her from Portland, Oregon, wanting her to join him. He had become fairly successful in the hotel business and had booked passage for her on a ship sailing from Belfast.

The ticket money had come too late, and Kathryn had missed the ship. But she had managed to secure passage on another.

In mid-Atlantic, the ship on which Kathryn was supposed to have sailed, sank.

There were no survivors.

When Kathryn finally arrived in New York, no one awaited her. Her father, certain that she had perished, had returned to Portland.

As twelve-year-old Kathryn sat alone on a bench near the huge registry room at Ellis Island, she gazed out at the magnificent Statue of Liberty. Even though she had no idea what was going to happen to her, Kathryn was no longer afraid as long as she could see the Statue of Liberty. She imagined that the Lady was protecting her.

Slowly the night passed.

There was no way to reach her father. He traveled continually and she did not have his address. She knew no one in America. And after paying for her passage, she had no money.

She had not eaten for two days, and as she quietly sat on the bench, she lay back looking at the Lady in the harbor.

Finally, one of the workmen on Ellis Island, a janitor, approached her and asked her name.

"Kathryn Brownly," she replied.

The man was amazed. His name was also Brownly—they were cousins.

She told him about her trip across the Atlantic. He offered to pay her fare from New York to join her father in Portland.

Kathryn Brownly finally found her father in Oregon. She went on to marry, to raise sons and daughters who became businessmen, farmers, nurses and teachers. Her grandchildren became civil administrators, lawyers, builders, engineers. Yet she never forgot her first experience in America. All her life she talked about the Lady who had protected her.

Lafayette had always believed that Liberty was the great hope of his countrymen and Laboulaye saw it as "enlightening the world."

But it was Emma Lazarus who perceived the power of Liberty in a woman's hand—her "Mother of Exiles"—who could protect and save the "tired . . . poor . . . huddled masses yearning to breathe free": those who had to flee because there was nowhere left for them to go, the victims of barbaric devastation, the lost, the bewildered, the threatened; and those, like the twelve-year-old Kathryn Brownly, who years later would become my grandmother, who simply needed to be taken in and cared for.

It is estimated that 85 percent of all living Americans are descended from someone who once passed by the graceful figure in New York harbor. To them she silently looked across, as she does today, with her illuminated lamp, heralding the prospect of an awaiting New World.

Bibliography

Angoff, Charles. *Emma Lazarus*. New York: Jewish Historical Society, 1979.

Bartholdi, Frederic Auguste. *The Statue of Liberty Enlightening the World*. New York: North American Review, 1885.

———. *L'Album du Bord*. Paris: 1879.

Betz, Jacques. *Bartholdi*. Paris: Editions de Minuit, 1954.

Chauffour, Felix. *Notices rétrospectives et recueil de souvenirs sur Colmar*. Colmar: Charles M. Hoffman, 1869.

Claretie, Jules. *L'Art et les artistes francais contemporains*. Paris: Charpentier, 1876.

———. *Peintures et sculpteurs contemporains*. Paris: Charpentier, 1873.

Cusset, Mercedes. "La Liberté éclairant le monde," *France-Amerique Magazine*. Paris: 1961.

Fischer, Carlos. *Colmar En France*. Paris: H. Floury, 1923.

Gauthier, J.B. "La Statue colossale de la Liberté," *Maison Monduit et Bechat, Gayot*. Paris: Gauthier et Cie, 1885.

Grad, Charles. *L'Alsace, le pays et ses habitants*. Paris: Hachette, 1889.

Koenig, Paul-Ernest. *La Vie en Alsace*. Strasbourg: 1934.

Laboulaye, Andrew de. *La Statue de la Liberté, 1886-1936*. New Haven, Conn.: Yale University Press. Vol. II, Spring, 1938.

Lazarus, Emma. *Emma Lazarus, Selections from Her Poetry and Prose*, edited by Morris U. Schappes. New York: Cooperative Book League, Jewish-American Section, 1944.

Le François, Philippe. *Paris souterrain*. Paris: Les Editions Internationales, 1951.

Menard, Rene. *L'Art en Alsace-Lorraine*. Paris: Librarie de l'Art, Charles Delagrave, 1876.

Price, Willadene. *Bartholdi and the Statue of Liberty*. Chicago: Rand, McNally and Company, 1959.

See, Julien. *Guerre de 1870*. Paris: Berger-Levvautt, 1884.

Seitz, Don C. *Joseph Pulitzer, His Life and His Letters*. New York: Simon and Schuster, 1924.

Swanburg, W.A. *Pulitzer*. New York: Charles Scribner's Sons, 1967.

Trachtenburg, Marvin. *The Statue of Liberty*. London: Penguin Books, 1976.